CLICK CLICK CLICK

From the Say My Name Series

Anne Varner

Karen DeVanie

Sugar Coated LLC

1st Round Edits by:
Andrea St. Amand
andreasaintamand.com

Publishing Assistance Provided by:
Michelle Morrow, M.S.
Publishology.net

Contents

To Momma, our biggest fan.

We based our book solely on our perspective, grounded in truth. We drew from investigative research and conversations with interested parties who prefer to remain anonymous. We have taken literary license where needed to enable the reader to better understand certain scenes.

Our hearts go out to anyone adversely affected by the events revealed in this story. We respect that murder ripples through families, friends, and communities, leaving permanent scars. The retelling of this case is an attempt to bring darkness to light and enable healing.

I don't understand why nobody talks about my brother anymore.

Kirk

Chapter One

The execution rolled across the walls of his bedroom

The first night was unbearable. He was in shock and panicking. Trying to sleep was a cruel joke. Every time he closed his eyes, the blinding flash and soul-piercing bang, followed by the odor of acrid smoke mixed with the sickening smell of gunpowder and flesh, haunted him. He longed for the respite of sleep to erase the pictures of the night. The living nightmare kept him awake when all he wanted was to drift into an endless sleep.

The execution rolled across the walls of his bedroom. The walls pressed in on him. He was trapped in an IMAX theater, a prisoner to his own horrendous deeds engulfing him in the wretched scenes playing in 3-D slow motion. Yet, his conscience would not let him wish it away or pretend it never happened. There was no escaping the reality of what they did.

The boy was in disbelief of the moment in his life. He couldn't reconcile who his parents raised him to be in their suburban town. His Christian family of do-gooders consisted of star athletes, successful students, active church members, future farmers, lawyers, and accountants. He was stuck between the image of how people saw him versus the mobster he wanted to be. The blank space between both worlds was where he executed the darkest of deeds.

He lay there, trapped in the prison of his mind.

How would he survive basketball practice tomorrow, preparing for the run at the State Championship and act normal? How could he sleep with the bag of bloody clothes stashed under his bed? The clothes breathed with the metallic, bloody stench of recent life. He envisioned the rotting flesh of his victim. He imagined the blood rustling in the plastic bag as it oozed. He needed to get under his bed to check it but was too terrified of the remains of a life he might find in the darkness. He lay there in silence and watched those movie images roll across his walls.

The victim's blood dripped from the ceiling at one point as he watched himself and his partner struggle loading the body. Desperate, he prayed to a God he pretended did not exist. Instead, God answered with every detail of the night flickering in his mind's eye--bang, flash, thud, smoke, fear, stench, ooze, wet chunks, silence.

Chapter Two

Nefarious doings came knocking

We close our eyes and can hear our childhood. We remember the conversations with our family unit, and we cannot forget the warm smells lingering from Momma's kitchen. At times we can hear a crack forming in the foundation.

Seemingly plucked from the series Twin Peaks, our sleepy mill town, Franklin, Virginia, with a population of 8,000 people, was rife with odd-ball characters and a noticeable local dialect. A man shot his estranged wife and her lover in the parking lot behind Daddy's drugstore when we were in elementary school. We watched him toss the murder weapon into a drain along the sidewalk as we walked with our Momma, who was on the way to make Daddy's deposit at the bank. That was probably the first time we discussed murder as a family.

Our mother testified at the disgruntled husband's trial.

It was a terrifying experience for her and for us.

Driven by fear, Momma asked if she could wear a disguise on the witness stand at the trial. We spent a week helping Momma pick the perfect, stylishly floppy hat, scarf, and sunglasses in case they granted her wish. Unfortunately, Momma never got to wear her Hollywood-style disguise, as her request was denied.

Thankfully, the man was convicted of his heinous

crimes. He was locked away and we didn't think of him again.

A short time later, a local business owner was assassinated in his jewelry store in the mid-morning hours. His name was Jack Smith. He was a friend, and we regularly frequented his family-owned jewelry store. That day, the devil himself, Willie Turner, walked in off the street carrying a shotgun in a pillowcase and wreaked havoc on Mr. Smith in the name of greed. He killed Mr. Smith in the store in front of customers and a local police officer. His killing started one more family conversation dealing with murder in our small community. Daddy could have been the target of such a senseless crime as he owned an independent drug store not far from Mr. Smith's store.

As curious teenagers, we would create reasons to go into the jewelry store after the murder. Spotting the blood stain on the carpet or the bullet rumored to still be lodged in the back wall was our mission.

In the early 1980s, murder hit closer to home. A tenth-grade classmate of Karen's killed a substitute mail carrier on an afternoon after school. Karen canceled plans to study for their Geometry exam with the boy before the end of school due to her priority of sun worshiping at the local country club. The boy kidnapped the young woman in her car with his hunting knife and savagely stabbed her. He was arrested the same night. Our parents broke the news to us the following morning. We got dressed, completed our morning routines and went to school. Karen took her exams, and we never mentioned it again. This was not a murder we discussed as a family. It was too close to home to imagine what could have been. We didn't discuss it until many years later as adults.

By the 1990s, we both moved away from town to pursue our futures. During one of our routine Sunday night calls with Daddy in the summer of 1992, he broke the news of another unimaginable crime. A local high school boy went missing a couple of years before. The news of a person in our social circle committing his murder stunned us. We read the local newspapers Daddy sent us in the mail, dumbfounded a deed as heinous as the premeditated, intentional execution of a high school boy could take place and go unsolved for such a long time.

In 1997, we thumbed through a People magazine and stumbled upon an article featuring an 88-year-old woman from Franklin, who killed her 52-year-old live-in boyfriend!

Si was hard to forget. She drove a red sports car with Washington Redskins (now the Washington Commanders) flags flying from her side mirrors. She usually wore short dresses and go-go boots. She was a real character and as sweet as can be. Shockingly, Si used a baseball bat to kill her boyfriend. She was the oldest woman in Virginia to be convicted of murder at the time. She served her time on house arrest. Surprisingly, the New York Post covered Si's story!

Murder was not the only crime on our family's minds. One night, nefarious doings came knocking on our door— not our house door, but Daddy's drug store. In the dark of night, thieves cut through three cinder blocks of the store's back wall and crawled through the bookkeeping office. They made their way to the pharmacy area and ran off with various drugs, watches, and cigarettes.

Next, they attempted to steal the cash register. Picture a non-electric, steal-based cash register with round push pegged buttons. Pushing the buttons in the right combination rendered a sale. They tried to open it but couldn't (all they needed to do was push the total button). They tried to pry open the steel drawer with scissors. The scissors were no match for a dinosaur cash register's reinforced steal money drawer. They hoisted the monster and tried to carry it through the hole in the back wall. Unfortunately for them, the gap was big enough for a grown man to crawl through but not big enough for Big Ole Bessy, the cash register. She was found lying on her side in the bookkeeping office next to the hole. Afterwards, we finally graduated to an electric adding-machine style cash register. We will never forget the endless fingerprint powder left after the police investigation. Luckily, the robbers never got to the drawer with the locked narcotics or the highly prized Spiro Agnew commemorative watches we kept well into adulthood.

On the one hand, it seems like forever since those times, and on the other, it seems like it was yesterday. They say hindsight is 20/20. When we look in the rearview mirror, sometimes we see a trail of horror woven into the town responsible for many of our childhood memories.

Chapter Three

The clicking blinker mimicked the sound of the gun's hammer

D riving home in a seemingly glass car, Mike exhibited the blood of his classmate inside his trunk for everyone to see. He didn't count on there being so much blood. It surprised him how it oozed around the tarp.

He could not focus on driving. He obsessively envisioned the blood in his trunk. If he slammed on the brakes, would a tsunami of blood crash into his back seat? It seeped toward him like a slow river of sticky tar.

Maybe Mike shouldn't have offered his car for the transport. He volunteered the vehicle purely because of spite for his family. The car was a gift from his mother the first Christmas they celebrated after his father died. Mike's rebellious heart interpreted the gift as a bribe. A bribe to compensate for his family keeping his dad's terminal illness from him until the last minute, robbing him of precious time he could spend with his father. What better way to sully his car than to put a dead body in it? Of course, his family could never know, but Mike would carry around the dark secret, a weapon which would permanently wound them if they ever found out.

His mind was going sideways. He was running late. He kept driving his see-through car, parading the blood through the streets. Every curve released another stream of blood flow. Turning into his driveway, the car's clicking blinker mimicked the click of the gun's hammer pulled back and forth.

He needed to find a way to quiet his mind so he could park the car and stroll into his house as if nothing happened. Somehow, he did. He walked in the front door and climbed upstairs to change his clothes, like a normal evening. The silence of the house and his mother's absence showcased his solitude.

He flipped on the light to his bedroom, and the reality of his actions popped on like a floodlight. He ran his hands along his pant leg, trying to brush off what felt like mud. It stuck to his fingers. It was not mud at all. The spongy gelatinous flecks of brain were now stuck on his fingers. The brain matter of his victim was splashed on his pants. He ran to the bathroom to wash his hands.

When he passed the bathroom mirror, he saw brain chunks in his hair. But as he clutched at his head, his fingers grasped only hair.

Blood and what he now realized was brain matter covered his pants and shirt. As much as he hated his mom, he couldn't throw his clothes in the laundry and force her to deal with his mess. He couldn't look her in the eye and lie. He would remove the spatter himself.

It wouldn't budge. The daunting task was taking too long. No matter how much he scrubbed, the stain got worse. As the water flowed from the spigot, it kept changing into a bloody waterfall. He closed his eyes and took a deep breath. But every deep breath brought in the nauseating copper odor. The do-it-yourself laundry plan was taking way too long. He finally gave up. He was on a schedule, after all.

He stashed the clothes in a bag, threw it under his bed, and jumped into clean clothes. He then retraced his steps, back downstairs, through the front door. He climbed into his car that was now his blood carriage and headed back into the Friday night.

He didn't want to drive through town and risk anyone catching onto his murderous deeds, but he needed to be seen.

Ironically, he really did not go out that much anymore. Still, tonight he needed to find a group of friends who would remember him partying with them.

He wanted to do nothing more than to drive to the police precinct and tell them what happened—no, tell them his part of the murder. What a conundrum!

The problem was, he couldn't tell what happened without implicating anyone other than himself. Back to the original plan. Get seen by several people.

Luckily, a group of girls stumbled through the threshold of a favorite secret drinking spot. Noticing their intoxication, Mike pulled to the corner, parked the car and joined in with the giggling, drunk clan. They bought it, or they didn't take note. Either way he appeared to be partying with friends.

Alibi established. No one would be the wiser.

Now he could get home and retreat to the haven of his bed. But soon, he would find the shelter he sought in the sleepy little town was his worst nightmare.

Chapter Four

Where in the hell is Franklin, VA?

F ranklin, VA, is a small town in the Tidewater region of Virginia. If you drive two hours south, you arrive in the Outer Banks of North Carolina. Virginia Beach is an hour or so to the east, and Williamsburg, Virginia is an hour north.

Franklin sits on the Blackwater River and has always been successful in the business of agriculture. The City of Franklin is adjacent to Southampton County. Southampton County is Virginia's top county in the production of cotton and peanuts. Pig farming is a lucrative operation in the county as well.

In the late 1800s, brothers from the locally rooted Camp family bought a sawmill on the Blackwater River. It was a small mill, but the Camp siblings turned it into a booming multi-million-dollar business. In the mid-1950s, the Camps merged with a bag and paper company in New York, forming Union Camp, a huge pulp and paper company. If you ever drove through or near a paper mill city, it's unlikely that you've forgotten the sulfuric smell of a mill. Anytime an outsider called our city stinky, we would tell them the offensive smell was, in fact, the smell of money.

The Franklin, VA, of our youth was a thriving paper mill city. If you came through on a particularly humid summer day, you might have seen white flakes falling from the sky.

That was no snowstorm, my friend. It was life in a paper mill city. One perk of living in the mill pollution was the free car wash in one of the parking lots where mill employees parked. As employees got off work, they could drive through the car wash and rinse the pollution from their cars. Sometimes, we would sneak into the lot and run our vehicles through the car wash. The car wash was not covered and offered no brushes, soap, or fun lights. It consisted of a bunch of metal pipes spraying water on your car as you rolled through. Even without the pomp and circumstance, we loved driving through under the cloak of night as if we stole a luxury car spa.

The Camp family pumped the fruits of their labor back into Franklin and paid their workers well. Although the paper mill has since been sold and considerably downsized, the Camp family name and generosity remain.

Paul D. Camp Community College was founded in 1970. The school sits on property the daughters of Paul D. Camp donated to the city. The campus opened to students in 1971. The community college still offers students degree programs, advanced skills, and trade pathways.

We both took ballet classes at the community college as youngsters. An instructor from a ballet school in Norfolk, VA, came a few times a week to teach students how to dance ballet and tap. We hated taking those classes, but Momma wanted us to have the experience and poise.

Momma enrolled us in a modeling class as teenagers. The instructor taught us how to pose for pictures, walk a runway, and choose what outfits to wear for a photo shoot. In addition, a professional came into the class for a session on makeup application for modeling events. We got our own photo session, resulting in slides we could turn into pictures. We chuckle when we think of the experience now, but it was a class we would have never gotten to experience if not for the generosity of the Camp family.

The YMCA in Franklin also came from the donations of the Camp family. Aptly named the James L. Camp, Jr. YMCA. We hold great memories of Halloween festivals, swimming lessons, and gymnastics at the YMCA. We referred to it simply as "The Y."

One memory we sisters share is our induction into the swimming pool as youngsters. We shared the same swim instructor and experienced a deathly fear of the diving board. To pass the polliwog class, students jumped from the diving board into the pool's deep end and swam to the ladder on the side. Now, for one to advance to a tadpole, a polliwog leapt independently off the scarily sky-high board and swam to the ladder. You could not pass the class without accomplishing the goal of flying high into the water. We girls are not failures. We are happy to report with much sputtering, crying, and shrieking, we successfully morphed into tadpoles. However, we both refused to jump into the pool from the board. Our instructor walked with us on the diving board and nudged us to jump. Each of us, on separate occasions, managed to pull the instructor into the pool as he tried to push us to jump. We feel confident he was grateful our family moved on to lessons at the country club.

Various celebrities visited Franklin throughout the years. As young girls, we remember the excitement over Elizabeth Taylor and Senator John Warner coming to visit. They stayed with one of the executives from the mill and his family. Luckily, they went to our church. On Sunday morning, seated in our designated church pew, we stared with open mouths as Elizabeth Taylor walked in with John Warner. She was absolutely gorgeous in person! Her smile brightened the whole church. Unfortunately, she was also a little unsteady on her feet as Bloody Mary's were the cocktail of choice before the church service.

Thank goodness we saw her at the beginning of church because we notoriously took communion and ducked through the back door. Instead of listening to the remainder of the service, we would go to the Dairy Queen down the street as the final prayer and hymn closed the service. These shenanigans did not sit well with our parents, but there was no stopping us. Momma was in the choir loft singing her heart out for the Lord. At the same time, Daddy was part of the Vestry. He managed the communion line, and he helped count the offering money after church.

By the final amens, our absence was noted.

Everyone knew everyone in Franklin, or so it seemed. If we didn't know you, we probably knew your people. If we didn't know your people, our daddy, the pharmacist, knew you.

We'll be the first to admit knowing everybody and their mailman's uncle came with advantages. For instance, when we went to have our cars filled with gas, we could tell the attendant to put it on our daddy's tab. We could walk into the local shoe store and get a pair of shoes with the simple request to charge them to our daddy. As members of the local country club, we could eat breakfast, lunch, and dinner by simply signing a piece of paper. One of us got to fly on a Union Camp private jet from the small municipal airport in Franklin to New Jersey and back.

Another advantage of living in a small town is the level of trust you develop with community members. As we mentioned, our daddy owned a drugstore right off Main Street. He was acutely aware of our customers' economic challenges. He established an unofficial barter system. Our cars got washed frequently, and our lawn was cut regularly by customers who traded these services for prescriptions. In the summertime, our back porch overflowed with Silver Queen corn, butter beans, tomatoes, and yellow squash.

We kept a little notebook at the register where we would write the customers' names and amounts, and Daddy would discreetly keep track. Once service was rendered, Daddy drew a single line through whatever transaction was complete. He never sent a bill to the names in the book beside the register. It was on the honor system with no pressure to settle the debts.

We worked as clerks, bookkeepers, and pharmacist's assistants in the drugstore. Working in the drugstore allowed us to interact with our community and get to know our neighbors. We spent afternoons stocking empty prescription bottles in drawers beneath the pharmacy counter, stocking shelves, organizing greeting cards, and wrapping Christmas and Valentine's candy. We also jumped at the chance to hand deliver prescriptions to the local shoe and jewelry stores. It was another opportunity for us to add things to Daddy's tab.

Unfortunately, Daddy also tried to train us to be soda machine engineers. One of our duties was stocking the machine according to the outer drink buttons and empty the coin bucket. To Daddy's chagrin and chuckles, we rarely got the drinks in the correct order. Usually, the change found its way to our pockets. Good news, this gave us carte blanche access to the drink machine key. Anytime we stopped in for a visit, we treated ourselves as well as our friends to to the nabs that lined the back counter and a cold bottle of Sundrop. In fact, we don't know the origin of the nickname 'nabs', but we continue to call them nabs no matter the manufacturer.

Knowing everyone in town also presented disadvantages.

As teenagers, we didn't get away with much. On one occasion, our parents bumped into a friend's parents at the local fair. They exchanged pleasant conversation, and they mentioned their son recently recovered from mono or what Momma called the kissing disease. They kindly told our parents to pass along a thank you to their daughter for the tutoring session for their son. It was kind of her to help him catch up on schoolwork while she was babysitting. Little did my friend's parents know mono also mysteriously hit our house.

One of us was busted and immediately grounded.

On another occasion, the chief of police pulled over one of us on the way to school for speeding. A stern lecture from the police chief ensued, but no ticket was given. Nice, right? Wrong.

After school, Daddy was waiting to speak of his encounter with the chief of police. He was kind enough to stop by the drug store to let Daddy know he stopped one of his daughters on her way to school and although he didn't give her a speeding ticket, perhaps Daddy should tell her to watch her speed. His kindness resulted in another daughter being grounded and losing driving privileges for a week.

Occasionally our parents left town and we threw parties. Most of them went great and were pretty low-key. However, a few of them got rowdy, resulting in a visit from the police. On the one hand, it was good because clearly, we lost control of the number of people at the party. Alternately, it was terrible because our parents heard there was a party because the officer mentioned it to Daddy at the drugstore. No amount of cleaning or groveling was going to save us. The worst part was the partygoers emptied every drop of the liquor from our home bar and we couldn't replace it. It was the last party in our house after we received our punishments.

Like most small towns, Franklin boasted several local hot spots where you went to be seen or to see about folks (gossip). As a local business owner, our daddy would meet with his crew at the Dairy Queen (DQ) before work. This was his way of hearing the actual happenings around town. These nuggets of information weren't necessarily covered in the newspaper. The coffee was weak, and the gossip was intense.

The local bar and tavern, Fred's, was and still is the site for a more exclusive meet and greet. At Fred's, your favorite waitress knows what you want before you take your seat. One of the owners is always at the bar to greet patrons with a hello. Fred's is more of a sit, let's talk politics and sports establishment. It has been a famous and beloved hot spot in Franklin. When you leave, you may feel the need to grab a tee shirt that says on the front, "Whereinthehellis-franklinva." On the back, it simply says, "Fred's," with a picture of Fred himself right there on the shirt.

It didn't matter which establishment you went to for your tittle-tattle; your awareness of the town scuttlebutt was more current than the local newspaper, the Tidewater News.

The town has changed since we lived there, and we don't get back there as often as we'd like. We can say one thing, you can take the girl out of Franklin, VA, but you will never take Franklin, VA out of these girls.

Chapter Five

It boggles the mind

T he first time we encountered Mike Jervey was at the local country club, Cypress Cove. The club members enjoyed tennis courts, a golf course, a swimming pool, and a restaurant. Most summers, we frequented the club daily.

Our daddy was big into golf. He worked six days a week but always found the time to hit the golf course. We learned to drive in the golf cart Daddy rented. We would let him ride from hole to hole if he was lucky. We made the golf course a no-rules zone. After Daddy finished his round of golf, he rewarded us with a pack of nabs and a cold bottle of Sundrop.

Momma was big into tennis with a group of friends we called "tennis ladies" who formed a team and traveled to different clubs to compete in tennis matches. We took tennis lessons at the club. There was a tennis pro who was on staff to teach the basics.

The way we became familiar with Mike was by watching him play tennis on those same courts. Of course, Franklin – and the country club – being so small, we knew of him and his family. His brothers are closer to our age.

But we remember watching Mike's tennis matches at the country club and saying, "Wow, he can really play!" Our own tennis lessons didn't pay off. We didn't take to the court in the same way Mike did. Instead, our talent was found lying by the pool and ordering hot French fries from the concession window.

Besides our seeing Mike play tennis at the club, we didn't know him. We didn't see him at parties or riding in town on the weekends. He went to the public high school and we went to the local private school, which meant we didn't see him at sporting or social events. Occasionally, we would see Mike's picture in The Tidewater News. He played basketball in one of the youth leagues at the YMCA and he played high school basketball. During basketball season, there was an extensive article regarding Mike and the Franklin High School team when Mike went against a high-ranking giant on the opposing team and successfully blocked a shot. It was exciting local news because Mike was far from tall and the player towered above him.

As part of the country club crowd, our families interacted with many of the same people as the Jerveys. We knew enough to understand Mike's family benefitted from affluence. Mike's dad, Louis Paschal "Packy" Jervey, worked for the local go-to insurance company, Manry Rawls, and served as President of the company in the 1980s. Mr. Jervey handled the insurance for Daddy's drug store thus we probably interacted with him more frequently than anyone else in the Jervey family. Mr. Jervey was a warm and personable man who was like an old friend.

Although we didn't run in the same circles as Mike, we and the Jervey boys experienced similar upbringings. We lived in friendly neighborhoods and our parents did well for themselves. It is unimaginable one of the Jerveys would be involved in a murder.

How does a well-rounded, affluent teenager transition from a country club tennis hot-shot and local high school basketball star into a diabolical schemer, contemplating the unthinkable act of taking someone's life? It boggles the mind.

You never know what's happening in a person's house. People put on masks at times in public and take those masks off at home.

Chapter Six

The dangerous conversations morphed into The Plan

Mike explored a rebellious phase. It was nothing unusual for a boy coming into his teen years as the youngest of five. There was no known abuse or neglect in his childhood, and Mike's family encouraged and honored him. He was purportedly not a troublemaker or a loudmouth. He did grow up in the shadows of a "bigger than life" dad and older brothers who were successful and highly praised. His rebellious streak stayed quiet in his heart, never really displaying itself outwardly.

Then, Mike imagined discord forming within his friend group. Some of these friends were rivals on the tennis court or in team sports.

As an athlete, Mike respected the competitive nature of sports and normally didn't let it affect his relationships with his peers. These are moments that could be lifted from any teenager's life.

A slight resentment crept in.

One night, Mike encountered harmless tomfoolery from within the ranks of his band of buddies. He felt a sting of treason, that he just couldn't shake. His friends toilet-papered his yard as a joke and Mike interpreted the prank as a betrayal of long-running friendships.

After the toilet paper incident, Mike looked outside his friend group and formed a friendship with a classmate named Fred Greene (no relation whatsoever to Fred's the beloved hot spot).

Sadly, life in the Jervey house took a tragic turn. Mike's dad was stricken with chronic pain that could not be relieved. Mr. Jervey was admitted to the local hospital in Franklin, where doctors ran a battery of tests and consultations. After almost a month, there were still no answers. Finally, he was discharged but was still in tremendous pain.

The tests came back either negative or inconclusive and Mike's parents decided the best course of action would be getting him down to Duke Medical Center in Durham, North Carolina. Mike remembers his parents leaving for North Carolina to find answers. Then, seemingly out of the blue, his brothers told him they needed to get down to Duke immediately to be with his parents because his dad was critically sick. When Mike arrived at Duke, his family told him his dad had cancer. Within weeks, without ever being discharged from the hospital in Durham, Mr. Jervey died on September 22, 1988, at only 54 years old.

In Mike's extreme grief, he became convinced that his entire family lied to him for weeks, perhaps even months, hiding his dad's illness from him and robbing him of precious time with his father. They must have underestimated him, judging he was too young to handle it.

Suddenly, his rebellion cracked open, flooding every bit of his heart and mind, turning him to pure hatred.

Mike stopped attending church and began skipping school. The once studious, respectful boy became indignant and hard and turned his loathing toward his mother.

He disconnected from his siblings, isolating himself, often spending long hours in his dark basement. The basement, having once been a game room in the Jervey home, where all the boys hung with their friends, became an isolation tank. Mike locked the door, played his music loudly, and brooded.

Only Mike and his mom remained in the house, both lost in their own seas of devastation and grief. Quickly, he turned his focus of loathing toward his mother, shutting her out of his life and only spouting angry, harsh language at her during the few interactions between them. He refused to hide or soften his bitterness toward her.

There was one friend Mike could count on--Fred.

Mike and Fred discovered they were kindred spirits, both angry towards the world around them. They formed a bubble of trust only with each other, agreeing that the world was against them, and that life was unfair and cruel. They fed off each other's resentment and cynicism toward everyone and everything. The hate they harbored individually, connected and grew, poisoning their minds, breeding deep mistrust and disrespect for life itself.

Dark talks formed inside their toxic bubble. Perhaps in order to regain their sense of personal power, Mike and Fred imagined what it would be like to be crime bosses in an underworld they created for themselves.

The lethal formula, coupled with rebellion and youth, made for a deadly cocktail waiting to be served. Then, an idea to commit the evilest of deeds was born. They pondered how it would feel to kill a human being.

Unfortunately, because Mike's mother and brothers were drowning in their own grief, Mike and his trusted friend went unchecked.

Fred's parents were estranged, and tensions ran high in the household. His mother worked hard at providing for and raising her sons. She assumed Fred was being a responsible teenager.

Taking advantage of their unchaperoned liberties the boys fell off the parental radars. The idea of murder took hold, and they frequently discussed their shared curiosity of how it would feel to kill. The dangerous conversations morphed into *The Plan*.

Chapter Seven

All they needed was to wait for the right victim

I n the isolated friendship bubble where Mike and Fred existed, the idea of bringing organized crime to Franklin, VA, sprang to life. Bringing in underworld businesses like drugs, weapons, and extortion gave them clout. By killing a person, they would become the kingpins of their dark universe, forcing people to obey and cooperate through fear or admiration. Once they committed a murder, it would be easier to recruit gang members, who they referred to as The Boys.

They started by stealing guns, enlisting local drug dealers, and seeking a target. Eventually, the occasional mention of killing became the focus of late-night discussions. These conversations were fueled by alcohol, drugs, and pure hatred of God, life, parents, and peers.

The snowball effect was quick and in-depth. First, there was the planning and discussions of how to pick a target. A viable victim was not hard to come by. Anyone who crossed them in any instance of disagreement landed on a list that was never written down but floated in the atmosphere the two shared. No one ever suspected that these two best friends were plotting to murder someone in their group. One false move at a party and any of those friends could land on the kill list. The untimely spilling of a drink, a casual disagreement, or accidentally excluding the duo from plans could get anyone killed. They even considered killing a police officer. Imagining what it would be like to end a life became their fixation.

Fred was streetwise and popular. He developed his disciplined work ethic from being raised by a father who was a prison warden. Seen as a leader amongst his classmates, Fred was the Drum Major for the Franklin High School Bronco Band. He also played soccer for the school. In their Senior Superlatives, Fred was voted Most Spirited because of his dedication toward FHS looking its finest and in encouraging all students to be involved in school activities, especially sporting events.

Mike was logical and organized. He was quiet and not considered part of the "popular crowd." Together, they made the perfect, quietly diabolical pair.

The entertainment of the evil deed turned into a full-on secret mission. They conspired to establish potential execution locations and scenarios. They discussed what could go wrong and the evidence they would need to contend with to ensure they didn't get caught.

The intense planning was way above what you would expect from teenage boys. In a time before graphic video games and crime scene-type television shows, their consideration was impressive.

The Plan was solidified before their Senior year started. They picked a field between two schools where construction was taking place. They intended to steal one of the blue plastic tarps from the construction site for the concealment of the body. They were confident by the time they lured a victim to the perfect spot. *The Plan* was as well-rehearsed as any professional mobster's. All they needed to do was wait for a suitable victim.

Like Dr. Jekyll and Mr. Hyde, Mike and Fred seemed to be everyone's buddy by day but could be their worst enemy on a random night. Diabolic duos are what many true crime documentaries and horror movies are based on today.

You never know who lurks in the shadows of the mask presented in public. Were these nice guys pretending to be murderers or murderers pretending to be nice guys? Either way, *The Plan* sprouted and matured into a life of its own, becoming a dark passenger who joined them at night as they rode through town looking for parties to attend.

Chapter Eight

Paula Deen meets Dateline

To: Sugar Coated Murder

From: Anonymous

Date: September 21, 2022

Subject: Your Podcast Coverage of my Case

"Greetings Karen and Anne. I am not real sure what exactly to say or even how I want to say it. I recently listened to your podcast..."

A s you can imagine, we read the email five more times before it was real. What was happening? And also, Yay! Another listener!

Throughout the next several hours, we went back and forth from *Should we be scared for our lives*, to *It's not every day you get to talk to a murderer*. From *Should we pack our shit now* to *How can we erase our presence on the world wide web*.

Did we mention we created a podcast? We picked the name Sugar Coated Murder because we needed comfort food to go along with our obsession with true crime.

To most of our family and friends, the two of us are an enigma. Way before reality TV, it was suggested to us on more than one occasion for a film crew to follow us every day and capture our creative weirdness.

One time, we took classes on how to become spiritual mediums. The participants and instructors did not prepare for the ensuing experience. Although mediumship was not our passion, we made lifelong friends and fell head-over-heels for our instructor's life force. We did not want to stop as the classes ended. As a matter of fact, we threatened to stalk the instructor from her studio's bushes as she gave clients personal readings.

Next, we tried our hands at improv classes. At the end of the course, there was a recital featuring our interactive skills. We sipped bourbon from our Tupperware containers in the parking lot before the show as a means of gathering our courage. We needed something to help us fight our fear of going on stage in front of a live audience. Again, we met wonderful people and made great friends, but never graced a stage since. We strive to find avenues of creativity to save our tired loved ones from our unending quirky personalities. We continue to seek outlets; be forewarned...

In late 2018, we started listening to a few true crime podcasts. We didn't know anything about podcasts or how to listen to one. By early 2019, our kids flew the coop giving us extra time in our days and nights. After listening to more true crime podcasts, we gathered plenty to discuss, especially a few hometown murders. We played with the idea for a few months and mentioned it to a few friends. We flipped back and forth about the subject of our podcast--true crime or our love of baking.

Our dear friend Andrea, a psychic medium in the

Charleston area whom we met through our class, did a group medium session we attended. After the reading, we shared a story regarding a murder in our hometown over Halloween Soul Cakes that Anne made. At the end of our story, Andrea declared we needed to create a podcast and tell stories of true crime, in the same tone we expressed at the gathering. In addition, she suggested we add a baking component because folks, including ourselves, would probably need comfort food to go along with the tales of true crime.

Our families supported us, happy we designed a platform to share the shenanigans of our youth and our sisterly banter. Ultimately, we threw our hats in the ring. Who are we to argue with a psychic medium? We purchased a $20 microphone from Amazon a week after the gathering.

Click, click, click. Is this thing on?

We then used our novice Google skills and researched ways to create a podcast. From there, we investigated murder cases from across the globe with a frenzied obsession. We hear our podcast has the vibe of Paula Deen meets Dateline.

We decided if we were putting out a true crime podcast, we wanted each crime thoroughly examined to ensure we told the story correctly. We would be in real trouble if someone ever looked at our online search history.

From day one, we showcase the victims in our cases, not the perpetrators. We are challenged by the information online because it shines a spotlight on the criminal and not the victim.

Court documents outline the crime and the primary focus is on the murderer. In our effort to recount pertinent information pertaining to the victims, we watch TV interviews and read obituaries. Occasionally, we get lucky, and the victims' friends or family communicate with us; still, it usually isn't until after we release the episode featuring their loved one.

One of the most common questions we get asked is, "How do you choose your cases?" Not to seem dramatic, but we feel the victims choose us. We seem to be spiritually drawn to certain cases. A chill from the universe assures us we found the right case to spotlight. Maybe we did pick up talent from our mediumship classes after all.

Highlighting the victims is an added challenge because of the imbalance of details. The victims and their families typically become a footnote because murder cases are sensationalized. In some instances, justice gets delayed or denied altogether.

The most challenging episodes transpire from the murder cases spun in our Virginia hometown. Because we hold such close knowledge of the subjects, we are pressured to tell the stories without interjecting our personal opinions.

Strategically covering the cases from our hometown puts us in a sticky situation. We certainly don't want to ruffle any feathers, but we're not ones to hold back on the truth.

Normally the macabre topic of heinous crimes does not bring humor, but comedic relief is our forte. Unfortunately, we tend to fumble and stumble between the legal jargon and the trial-related technicalities. We laugh at ourselves, otherwise we would turn off the microphone and walk away. Add a titch of boozy spirits to the mix, and the dark humor appears. We trim the more inappropriate humor during editing. Still, we can't help but leave in a little organic laughter, which captures our true selves. Most times, we apologize to Momma for our salty language as it continues to inexplicably fall from our mouths.

It didn't take us long to know we needed comfort from the loathsome actions we recount. Enter our love of baking.

We grew up baking treats in Momma's kitchen from the time we were knee-high to a grasshopper right through to today. We came up with the name Sugar Coated Murder because a good southern cook knows comfort food heals the soul. God knows these victims and their loved ones need comforting and healing. As we bake on our episode, we comfort ourselves and our listeners, who might find the subject matter disturbing. We genuinely want listeners to feel like they're sitting in the kitchen with us discussing true crime and baking.

We released our first podcast the following January of 2020. We imagined maybe 10-15 people would listen, mainly our friends and close family. A few short years later, we've recorded over 100 episodes and are still going strong with 40,000+ downloads.

Fast forward to September 21, 2022, when we received the email with the subject line "Your Podcast Coverage of my Case." Before we noticed the "from" line of the email we wondered if maybe we received an email from beyond the grave and then we feared our little home-baked podcast landed us on a kill list.

Chapter Nine

Nobody knew there was a kill list

Mike and Fred created the list by identifying males they felt opposed them. They sorted their peers into two categories: the recruitable or the opposition. The pair derived the kill list from the opposition.

If anyone cracked a joke and it landed the wrong way, the jokester was added to the kill list. A wink at a girl one of them liked and the winkster took a number in the kill list line. The longer the recipient stayed there, the more chance to be selected as the target. A genuine apology removed a potential casualty from the list, all the while clueless to the existence of the game.

The twosome scrutinized the targets for accessibility. Could you be easily convinced to go to a location with the two of them? Did you carry weapons? Did you fit into their timing? For example, an athlete's schedule caused maneuverability obstacles.

Killing an officer of the law would be the creme de la creme of murders and would give them the street credibility they deserved. But they couldn't configure how to avoid the risk of him pulling his gun on them, so he didn't fit the criteria. None of these people possessed any idea how close they came to death.

Mike and Fred identified the target and set *The Plan* in motion before time allowed him to remove himself.

Chapter Ten

The sound was his own heavy breathing

"Tonight's the night," he told himself as he pulled his jacket closed to ward off the chill. As for the pit in his stomach, he didn't know whether it was from dread or excitement. As he mindlessly filled his car with gas, he reviewed the checklist. Did they consider everything?

Inside the car Fred mentally checked off his preparations. Blue tarp acquired. Gun loaded. Shovels secured in trunk.

The mission was planned down to the tiniest of details. They identified dumpsters where they could dispose of items from the crime scene—a different dumpster for each item. Mike rehearsed his to-do list for *The Plan* and Fred's as well. Get it done quickly and efficiently.

His concentration was broken by the distinct aroma of onion rings wafting through the crisp night air. He turned his gaze across the street to the busy parking lot of the local Dairy Queen in time to catch a glimpse of a familiar car. Were his eyes playing tricks on him or was it really the target? Yes, it was the target in the drive-thru line waiting for his order. Did he know he was waiting in line for his last meal?

Maybe there was still time to stop *The Plan*. Part of him didn't want it to happen.

They tucked away the illegally acquired gun for the right opportunity to execute the mission. A mission to establish their mobster status in town. Fred found his favorite, a .357 magnum, at the home of his on-again-off-again girlfriend's and permanently borrowed it. When the seniors submitted their Christmas wish lists for the high school newsletter, Mike wished Fred would finally get the chance to use Magic, their secret nickname for the .357 magnum.

The target left DQ and headed toward the designated spot in town.

It's Go Time.

With a full tank of gas, Mike and Fred drove to the designated meeting spot, a small shadowy area between an elementary school and a middle school. The music thumped in Mike's car, but their minds remained focused on their task. They didn't talk. *The Plan* reflected the loyal bond the two formed over the year. Their bond propelled them into the darkness.

The target pulled in soon after they arrived at the prearranged meeting place under the guise of working out their differences. The three started idle chit-chat, and Mike thought, "Nah. We aren't gonna do this."

The chatter fell silent as something banged at the back of the school. Was someone else there? Was the clatter the sign Mike wished for?

Mike volunteered to check the noise location. As he walked through the cold darkness, the sound in his ears was his own heavy breathing. He was torn between wanting to find no one in the dim spot and finding anyone who would put an end to the nefarious plan.

Walking away in the opposite direction was not an option, because there was no way he would leave his friend there. Fred was his ride-or-die to the bitter end. He would never walk away. He would push through and prove he was worthy of their friendship. He wanted to convince himself he was mobster material, destined to rule the world of crime in their tiny, insignificant town.

Left alone with the target Fred considered putting Magic to work before Mike returned. But he didn't want to rob his friend of being part of the killing. They planned it together. It was only right to share the experience.

The noise was benign. Mike returned from confirming nobody was hiding in the dark and they started comparing their favorite bands' music. The boys sat in the target's car, listening to his tapes. Mike thought maybe the mood shifted. The distraction of the noise was surely a sign *The Plan* wouldn't happen tonight.

They walked to check out a tape in Mike's car. As they left the target's car, Mike heard himself whisper, "If we are gonna do this, do it now, so we can get out of here."

What did I hear Mike say? At first Fred thought Mike indicated he wanted to leave, put a stop to *The Plan* and then he realized his friend had given him the green light. *Let's do this.*

Was that what he meant to say? The mood darkened. Mike wanted to escape the shifting mood and *The Plan.*

They walked to Mike's car to find the tape, still discussing music, sharing what each of them liked and recently discovered.

The mood shifted again.

The target sensed something heavy was getting ready to happen, like maybe he made a mistake by showing up alone. He was in over his head. He mentioned that perhaps they could negotiate a deal for the weekly payments.

Fred responded, "It's too late for that now." He taunted the target. Saying it was a spooky night and "you never know what could happen out here alone." The silence already enveloped the night. It was creepy enough. Why did Fred make it worse?

And what was the other noise? Was Fred cocking and uncocking the gun?

Click

Click

Click...

Chapter Eleven

Soulful brown eyes

The Whitleys reported their son Trent missing on Saturday, February 24, 1990. He did not sleep in his bed and none of his friends encountered him the previous night. He always called if he made plans to stay out past curfew or at a friend's house.

Raymond Trent Whitley was born June 19, 1972. He was a typical Gemini with an exuberant personality. Trent was the youngest of four boys with an adventurous nature. He was playful, easygoing, and adored by his brothers.

His mother, Delores Whitley, shared a story with the local newspaper during the investigation into Trent's disappearance. The story speaks to his fearless nature at the age of two years old. While Mrs. Whitley was doing housework and Trent's dad was in the garage doing chores, Trent wanted to go outdoors. His mom opened the door, let him toddle into the yard, and yelled to her husband Trent was headed his way. She went back inside and continued her housework.

Later, she went outside to check on Trent. She asked her husband where Trent was because he wasn't standing close. Apparently, Trent dodged his father.

Mr. Whitley did not hear Mrs. Whitley yell to say Trent was coming outside. They discovered the gate to the fence was opened, and Trent was gone. Mrs. Whitley ran to the neighbors' houses frantically searching for him, but no one noticed the little boy.

The couple drove around in a panic looking for their son. Mrs. Whitley sent Trent's three older brothers to scan the neighborhoods to find him.

Finally, a police car pulled into the Whitley's driveway. Two-year-old Trent was proudly perched in the car. He made it several neighborhoods away before the police officer spotted him and returned him safely to his parents.

Being from a rural town in the south, it's no surprise Trent developed a love for the outdoors. He enjoyed boating and water skiing. He developed a real passion for hunting. Due to his devotion to hunting, he was granted an age waiver to a local hunt club when he was seventeen. The special permission was a big deal in a Southern county where the first day of deer season was a national holiday.

Trent disappeared when he was a seventeen-year-old honor student in his senior year at Franklin High School. He wasn't into athletics, but he briefly participated in the band. Trent wasn't loud or boisterous; yet he was far from an introvert. None of his plethora of friends spoke a negative word about him to us.

He was excited for graduation and the end of the school year. In the weeks before he disappeared, he modeled his cap and gown for his family with pride. He didn't know exactly what he wanted to do after high school. He enjoyed working outdoors and seemed to love working part-time at the sod farm. Trent spent a lot of time with his girlfriend. He stayed busy going to high school, working his part-time job, and of course, hunting.

By all accounts, Trent was a typical teenage boy thriving in Smalltown, USA. Trent's mom told news reporters he was a good boy and didn't give his parents any real problems. She explained he wasn't perfect, but he spent a lot of time with his family, and he obeyed his parent's rules. A great picture in Trent's high school yearbook shows him and his date at a formal dance. Trent is wearing a tuxedo, with a rosebud boutonnière, and he's holding a drink. His engaging smile plastered across his face illuminates the picture. His wavy dark hair is fixed, and his dark eyes are bright. He has a little bit of a cool mustache going. He is handsome and happy, and his date is quite smitten.

His senior picture is more serious. He isn't smiling, but you can see those soulful brown eyes, the same cool mustache, and stylish haircut. In the same yearbook is a candid picture of Trent in class with his peers sitting close to him. He obviously doesn't know the photograph is capturing the moment. Trent is comfortable in the classroom, surrounded by his classmates. His signature smile beams from the photograph.

How does a vivacious, well-liked small-town boy get

caught on the kill list of two wanna-be-mobster classmates? Was it as simple as a casual disagreement in a confined classroom?

In mid-February of 1990, during History class, Fred tried to convince Trent to pay a $10 weekly fee for "protection". Trent didn't take Fred seriously and didn't give weight to the silly request.

A few weeks later, during History class, Fred demanded the protection money from Trent, who flippantly responded with a chuckle saying, "I don't owe you any money. I don't need your protection."

Fred was infuriated with Trent's words and their delivery. *Who does this kid think he's talking to!* The exchange led to the biggest event of Trent's young life.

After history class, Fred followed Mike into his next class and launched into a tirade which caught Mike off guard. In front of the whole class and possibly the teacher, Fred proclaimed for all to hear he was going to kill Trent Whitley. And in the blink of an eye, the kill list grew.

No one that witnessed the exchange revealed Fred's threat on this cold February day. When Trent went missing ten days later, not one person disclosed the outburst to authorities, to the newspapers, or to Trent's family.

Chapter Twelve

No more hellos, no more goodbyes

February 23, 1990. A mundane Friday in Franklin. Perhaps a bit quiet. No significant sporting events on tap for the night.

After school, Trent Whitley headed to his part-time job at the local turf and sod farm. He went home after work, showered, and joined the family for dinner. Trent and his mom discussed a recent trip she took.

He finished dinner and departed for his night with friends. Because it was cold, his mom reminded him to grab a coat. Trent told her about the two coats in his car. Then he was gone.

No more hellos. No more goodbyes.

No more reminders to bundle himself against the cold night. Gone.

When Trent's mom awoke the next morning, Trent's bed was still made from the night before. Mrs. Whitley called around to his friends as panic set in, but no one noticed him the previous night. A few friends mentioned they planned to connect with him, but he never showed. As Trent's mom bolted out of the house, she spotted her son's car in the park across the street. Someone left the windows open and his keys hanging in the ignition.

All signs trouble was afoot.

She noticed one of Trent's coats and a box of cassette

tapes on the back seat. It was time to call the police. Something terrible happened to her son.

A police officer came to the Whitley home to take their statements. He called a tow truck to haul Trent's car to the police impound lot. Trent's case was assigned to an investigator, who happened to be out of town for two weeks. The unprocessed car sat in the impound lot with the windows still open.

But wait, did no authorities search for Trent the entire two weeks the investigator was gone? Was anyone taking the missing boy's case seriously?

Upon his return, the detective immediately began a deep dive investigation into Trent's whereabouts and ordered a forensics technician to process Trent's car. They found no evidence of interest in the vehicle. No one knew Fred, the boy who pulled the trigger and ended Trent's life, lounged in the backseat the night Trent died.

The investigator interviewed hundreds of classmates and students from Franklin High School; the police department established a tip line for anyone with information. Eventually, the department posted a $5,000 reward as incentive for anyone who might have details.

The team of detectives thoroughly vetted thousands of tips. A self-proclaimed psychic came from another town and presented the investigator with a hand-drawn map of where she predicted Trent's body could be found. She couldn't give any details as to the exact location of the wooded area, but she was certain it was near a body of water.

Several of the interviewed students mentioned Trent intended to meet three of his friends and party at the local hotel. With names in hand, the investigator called each friend into the police station to be interviewed.

The first boy came in, answered questions, gave details of the expected events for the night of the disappearance, and agreed to take a polygraph test, which he passed.

The second boy hesitated to go to the police station. He didn't show for his appointed interview time, so the investigator drove to the boy's job. Mr. Hesitator got a free ride to the police station. He answered questions and gave details of the night but did not pass the polygraph due to high anxiety.

In the meantime, a third boy got wind of the free rides being given to the police station and the personal quiz shows. He quickly lawyered-up and was never given a polygraph. All three of Trent's friends told the same story. The boys made plans to go to a party with Trent; he was a no-show, and they went without him, expecting to see him in the crowd.

The boys remained persons of interest throughout the

search for Trent and stuck to their story until the end. Despite the thorough investigation, no one harbored any suspicion about Fred or Mike, the boys who ended Trent's life.

Chapter Thirteen

They worked in tandem to roll the body from the ditch

B ang!
    Neon blue flashed in his eyes. Followed by the loudest crack Mike ever heard. He jerked around in time to see the body hit the ground.

Holy Shit! It was done. *The Plan* was in motion.

Holy Shit!

The voice in his head yelling, "Holy Shit," repeatedly.

Was he saying it aloud, or was it in his head? *Am I hallucinating?*

Fred's hands grabbed his shoulders to steady him. "Hey! We came here to do a job, so let's finish it." Fred's voice was firm, calm.

Moving forward, Mike never gave another regard to the target as a human being. He focused on completing his task. His self-preservation demanded he keep a one-track mind to finish the job.

The reality of stealing a 17-year-old boy's life was not a consideration. He became the target because he fell for their ruse to lure him to a clandestine spot between the two schools. No regard to the inevitable suffering of the target's parents, brothers, or friends.

The next steps in *The Plan* dictated erasing the evidence and cleaning up the crime scene. Autopilot kicked in as they got to work.

The first task was daunting: lugging the body into

Mike's trunk. They laid the tarp they had stolen on the ground beside Trent's barely cold body. Next, they maneuvered the body into position by half dragging/half lifting him. Neither noticed the growing pool of blood and scattered flesh beneath their shoes. Once the body was on top of the tarp, they folded each side over, wrapping it around him. Surprisingly, getting the bundle into the trunk presented unforeseen problems. It took multiple clumsy attempts. The limpness of the body caused issues every time they tried to lift him. The tarp slipped and a leg or an arm started to roll out, so the boys would stop, lay the body down and readjust the tarp. They hoisted the package in unison more than once to clear the edge of the trunk. *He wasn't heavy in life, but he is heavy in death.*

After securing the body in the trunk, Mike and Fred drove away in separate cars. They crept through town— Mike in his glass car, Fred driving the target's vehicle with the windows down so the night air kept him in the zone. They took different routes so they would not be seen together.

They'd planned to ditch the victim's car at the park on Meadow Lane. The park was rumored to be a popular spot for drug deals, which would help nudge the narrative. Perhaps their victim met with a couple of bad guys. Bad dudes who did a terrible thing to him. In addition, it threw suspicions away from the partners and helped prove they hadn't seen the target.

Mike drove to the meeting place next to the park and pulled his car into a dark, out-of-way space. He waited for Fred to wipe the prints from Trent's vehicle. Mike's car was as silent as a grave—no chatter, no music—but his thoughts screamed. Unexpectedly, he couldn't remember why he agreed to participate in such a vile deed. He couldn't stop recounting. *How did we get this far? Why didn't anyone stop us?*

The reality washed over him. *The Plan.* The killing. The evil. The finality. Irreversible.

Fred went to work erasing any clue of them hanging out in Trent's car. No trace left behind. *I should have grabbed a towel from home. Ah, Dairy Queen napkins. I knew I'd seen them when I was in the back seat earlier.* He methodically wiped and double wiped the steering wheel, the ignition, the steering column and the seats where he sat before and after the execution. Fred left the target's car windows down and keys in the ignition then jumped into Mike's car shoving the napkins in his pocket. Silent. Grinning.

As they were pulling away, Fred's girlfriend motored by with her best friend. Somehow, she didn't see them. The close called revved Mike's paranoia

Mike asked Fred, "What went through your mind as you pulled the trigger?"

Fred replied he thought of Mike and doing him proud.

Mike did not expect his answer. The response was odd and out of character. Mike was sure his mind was a blackhole, devoid of human emotions. The reverberation of the bang erased Mike's cognizance. As the fog cleared, Mike focused on what came next and how he couldn't just back out at the last minute.

As Mike pulled off the main road toward the farm, he realized in an instant he didn't remember driving there. In a flash he stood by the trunk as Fred handed him a shovel. Did the shovel materialize out of thin air?

Of course, it didn't. As part of *The Plan*, they purposefully transported the shovels to Mike's family-owned farm. They marched to the pre-designated digging area, just yards away from the threshold of the cabin.

The night was cold, but the ground was not frozen. Even so, Mike's shovel could not penetrate the soil. His accomplice easily controlled his shovel. Mike realized he was in shock, physically frozen into place. He knew it was a two-person job, and by not digging he risked the entire remainder of *The Plan*. His body refused to go through with what needed to be done.

We've come all this way and now he's shutting down? Did we need to practice shoveling? Frustrated with Mike's sudden inability to move dirt with a shovel, Fred proposed the duo dig a shallow grave and return on Sunday to dig a deeper hole.

Silently they recovered the body from the trunk, gathering tarp and body parts as best they could. Once again, they clumsily hoisted the package over the bottom ledge of the trunk. They half carried/half dragged the tarp and corpse to the hole, barely a ditch. *Come on Mike. You're slowing us down. I've done all the digging. Now I have to do the carrying myself?* Fred was carrying and Mike was dragging. Tucking the tarp around the limp, bloody body, ensured no clothing or flesh stuck out. In the pitch black, they gathered tree branches, limbs, and leaves. They made sure to completely cover the shallow grave so no blue from the tarp could be seen. They calculated the risk of leaving the job unfinished against the risk of no alibi. Sticking to the schedule, the pair drove back to town. You must be seen, right?

The thunderous music broke the somber mood. Fred excitedly asked if Mike was aware of their power.

Mike guessed aloud that their power came from having gone through with it, sticking to *The Plan.*

Fred corrected him. They gained power by possessing sole knowledge of the homicide. Mike gazed through the windshield at the starry sky and pondered, *God knows.*

There it was.

His new claim to being an Atheist lasted forty-five

minutes. Back at the pre-arranged spot between the two schools, he convinced himself he wasn't going to Hell because God no longer existed. No God, no Hell.

His heart told him loud and clear God indeed existed, and He saw exactly what they did. Mike was going to Hell for it, and he would surely go insane on the way there.

Except for only half-burying the body, they mastered all *The Plan*'s steps so far. Mike did not need to remind himself what else needed to be done to complete the mission. They trained for it hundreds of times.

Feeling his mood lifting, Mike triumphantly dropped Fred at his home. Fred slammed the car door. *I hope Mike pulls it together. Do I need to formulate a new plan?* And the two parted for the night. Once Mike established his alibi with the drunk girls downtown, after he gave up on washing the execution out of his clothes, he collapsed into bed. He wasn't the smug mobster he expected to suddenly become. Instead, he fell into a morbid carnival in his mind, into warped memories of blood, the weight of the body, the unruly limp limbs, a shoed foot flopping out of the tarp, elbow jutting into his rib, matted hair, all on an endless carousel rolling around his bedroom walls.

Finally, Saturday came. He could go to practice and leave it all on the court. Distracting himself would be a relief. As he gathered his gear for basketball and steadied himself to get back in his car, Mike recalled the target wearing a hat and glasses on Friday night. He distinctly remembered the items thrown into the ditch at the farm did not include the cap and eyeglasses. Leaving any evidence behind risked exposure.

Mike called Fred. He told him about his basketball practice schedule and ordered Fred to retrieve Trent's hat and glasses immediately, before anyone discovered them. Trusting his friend would accomplish the critical mission promptly and discreetly, Mike left for basketball. Blasting his music, in hopes of keeping his mind from looping back to the night before, he sped off to the YMCA.

Once at practice, he focused on drills, plays, and free throws. Mike was steady on his feet until a teammate ran past him with the stench of last night's alcohol seeping from his sweaty body. He retched, fighting back vomit. The smell of alcohol in the blood and brain matter from the night before rushed back to him in a flashback.

Mike didn't expect blood and brain to smell of alcohol. He did not know it takes 30 seconds for alcohol to reach the brain once consumed. If the victim consumed half a beer before he met, it would have moved to his brain via his bloodstream and mixed in with the spatter, gushing from the gunshot wound.

Nor did he predict the encounter with his teammate, hungover and sweating it out to once again remind him of what they did. Karmic proof he was never going to get away from the darkness. Losing his mind was guaranteed.

As Mike practiced free throws at the line, in walked Fred. The baseball cap and glasses donned by his cohort did not overshadow his proud grin. Mike nearly passed out. How dare Fred try to pull off a private joke! The act weighed on Mike's mind, reminding him there was no way he would escape the ensuing insanity. Presently, he might not survive practice.

And then a final doozy. At the end of practice, Trent's girlfriend approached Mike and Fred. She asked if they connected with him last night and said he mentioned meeting them around 8pm. Uncharacteristically, Trent ghosted her on their plans for the evening.

Mike braced himself. *Here we go. The first test is here. I better get it right. Dress rehearsal is over.*

Mike followed the script exactly. Trent intended to meet with them at the Community College to buy them alcohol because he owned a fake ID. They waited for him for 15 minutes, and he never showed. Frustrated they left and went their separate ways. He never called them either.

She bought it. Mike passed the first test. Sanity beamed back in sight.

Maybe he could make it through the darkness after all.

Sunday morning Mike awoke with new resolve. He and Fred would accomplish their grim task of moving the body to a deeper grave. More digging and touching Trent's lifeless body. The last place he wanted to be was back at the cabin, exposed to the cold air and the stark reality of the slaughter.

He hoped he could handle the job better now since a little time passed. He looked at it as a job. He would stay focused and persevere. It was a risk to dig a second grave in the light of day, but better excuses were plausible on a sunny Sunday afternoon as opposed to a Friday night.

Upon arrival, they launched into their task, mostly quiet, except for a bit of idle chitchat. For the new grave, they picked a spot under a big oak tree in the front yard of the cabin not far from the pond. They dug for hours and cleared a four-feet deep grave. Next, they cleared the debris used to cover the ditch Friday night. And there it was, the body still tucked into the bloody tarp. As soon as Mike reached for the blue plastic, ice-cold fear overcame him. He envisioned Trent reaching out and grabbing them while they tugged at the material.

He worried the stench would assault his senses when they moved the body. He couldn't vomit and risk looking weak in front of Fred. He hesitated long enough for Fred to grasp the tarp first. Strong-minded Fred only wanted to get their chore over with and get on with his day, so he did not have to think about Trent anymore.

Holding it at each end, they worked in tandem to roll

the body from the ditch like a log. Trent was still heavy; hence the two boys clumsily dragged him to the grave. As they pulled, the tarp unrolled, exposing parts of their dead classmate. Fred reached into the tarp and rifled through Trent's pants pockets for his wallet. He helped himself to the $200 in cash and threw the wallet into the grave. They might as well make some money in this transaction and Trent no longer needed it. All Mike wanted was to complete the mission and get out.

It was too risky to abandon the tarp with the body because the tarp might be easily spotted if anything shifted. With a big shove they rolled Trent's body away from the tarp and into the grave, to his final resting place.

Thud. The sound would resonate in Mike's mind for many coming months. They shoveled the dirt over the body, then covered the grave with debris from the wooded area by the cabin. Silently, they left, finally having completed their morbid task.

Chapter Fourteen

Somebody knew something

The rumor mills ran rampant through Franklin. Perhaps Trent met with trouble and went on the lam. Some predicted a gang kidnapping. All agreed Trent was nowhere to be found.

Vigil after vigil was held for Trent. The Whitleys gave interviews with statewide media outlets, doing their best to keep a spotlight on the case. They were desperate to know what happened to their precious son. The police came up with no solid leads, merely dead-end tips. The investigator and his team traveled throughout Virginia and multiple states to interview people who reported seeing Trent. Unfortunately, every painstaking trip led to a disappointing dead end.

In June of 1990, Trent's class graduated without him. As his classmates left town to pursue their futures, the list of available witnesses in Trent's last days diminished significantly. The investigation stalled. Trent's disappearance was never classified as a cold case because it stayed active.

Watching Trent's classmates move on with their lives was excruciatingly hard for the Whitleys. Trent's cap and gown remained unused in his bedroom, hopefully waiting for his return. For two years, on the anniversaries of Trent's disappearance, the Whitleys spoke to reporters and rehashed their plight.

Time and time again, Mrs. Whitley would say she strongly believed somebody knew information, but out of fear they did not tell the police.

Little did the entire town know what happened to Trent. No one developed an idea Mike and Fred murdered Trent and pressed forward with their lives right under their noses.

As time marched on, Mrs. Whitley told reporters the family reconciled in their hearts their adventurous, kind, and loving son and brother would not be coming home. Yet they assured themselves he would walk through the front door one day and prove them wrong.

Some of Trent's closest friends visited the Whitley home often, sitting at the kitchen table with Mrs. Whitley, supporting the family. Knowing his friends continued to care gave her comfort. The lead investigator formed a close bond with the Whitley family and continued to keep them informed of any new information. Their bond continues today.

Chapter Fifteen

He swirled in panicked disarray

The Monday after the killing, the school week started, along with more basketball practices. The more time separated Mike from the crime, it became easier to ignore his gruesome reality. The murder haunted his dreams a little less with each passing night. He avoided thinking of Trent. He fixated on how he and his best friend achieved the ultimate act of killing, covering it up, and getting away with it. Forever bonded.

The bonded pair now schemed to gain the credibility they needed while keeping their secret between them, balancing power and silence and how to use them to their best advantage.

The town searched for the missing high school senior. Mike and Fred appeared concerned and involved. They volunteered to post missing person flyers then found ways to get out of going through with it. They told their classmates they'd see them at the vigils held in the park across from the Whitley's home, the same park where they abandoned Trent's car. But the pair never attended any vigil.

News articles appeared on a regular basis, including interviews with Trent's mom. Mike and Fred tried to fade into the background. They avoided reading the news articles where Mrs. Whitley repeated her theory someone knew important details and concealed it from the authorities.

But Mike couldn't avoid a local reporter. She was constantly on the beat, trying to sniff out clues as to what happened to the Whitley boy. Desperate to help solve the mystery and be the first to scoop the story, she asked many questions. She called Mike about one month after Trent's disappearance. The reporter heard Trent planned to meet up with Mike and Fred that fateful night. She prodded why were they meeting. What was the plan after they were supposed to meet Trent? Was Mike sure he never had contact with him on Friday? She pressed him on the phone for several minutes. But he stuck with the story they formulated as part of *The Plan*.

After the exchange with the reporter, Mike called Fred. Fred told him to voluntarily go to the police station and repeat their story. Mike obeyed and drove his still-bloodstained car downtown, parked in the police lot, and walked inside.

He conveyed to an officer that he and Fred were supposed to meet up with Trent the night of the disappearance, and he wanted to set the record straight. Policemen greeted Mike with open arms and pats on the back. Again, Mike told his rehearsed story, and they took him at his word.

It was as if the police assumed credibility from Mike's

last name alone. No boy from a prominent, good-standing family could be involved in anything heinous.

If they pushed him a little bit, perhaps they would notice beads of sweat bursting forth onto his brow. The right question in an assertive tone may unleash a confessional flood. No one could tell, but Mike teetered on a cliff's edge. He wrestled with how to confess the crime without implicating Fred, all while telling their cover-up tale.

On the outside, Mike appeared calm and helpful. On the inside, he swirled in panicked disarray, knowing the coagulated, crimson stain on the carpeting of his trunk waited to be discovered. They missed the opportunity to confiscate the car which carried Trent's murdered body away from the crime scene. The police took Mike's story at face value, thanking him for volunteering to assist in the investigation.

Later in the day, Fred stopped by to speak with police officers as well. His story did not match Mike's, but the officers never questioned either of the boys further. After all, Fred was the best friend of the boy raised by good citizens of Franklin. Affluence and connections through friendship protected two cold-blooded executioners. The high of fooling the investigators distracted Mike from the detour Fred took from the rehearsed story of *The Plan*. But a seed of doubt was planted.

The exchange with the authorities gave the duo a more considerable boost of confidence. Their dark secret was safe. Mike and Fred gained the power and respect needed to run their organized crime operation. They sustained no worries of being caught, especially with graduation getting closer and closer. It was a running joke between them. The town was in their clutches, and no one was the wiser. *The Plan* had gone smoothly thus far, and everything was working in their favor. The combination of his colleague's street smarts, and Mike's privilege of carte-blanch family credibility was building a shelter of protection.

As Trent's family lived in anguish, Mike and Fred moved on with their young lives with little worry and unapologetically inflated egos. As the town continued searching for answers to the mystery of a 17-year-old boy who disappeared without a trace, his killers ran the roads, and partied at will.

But why did Fred deviate from the agreed-upon story they rehearsed countless times? This first inkling pulled at Mike's confidence. Maybe he and his accomplice were not on the same page after all. More seeds of worry emerged as well. His paranoia never stopped.

Why did it feel like the paranoia was the loudest when it was quiet? It was always in the back of his conscience tapping at him, reminding him he would never be safe from what he did. Still the haven of his bedroom was turned into a fun house of images flashing across the walls. The blue flash, the loud bang, the thud of Trent's body hitting the ground, the stench, and the brain matter on his pants came flooding back at the most unexpected times. The silence of sleep was torturous for Mike. The guilt of what he participated in was always lurking in the murky corners of his mind. The weight of knowing he could never betray his friend or let his family know what a terrible person lived in their midst was soul-crushing. He swore people secretly scrutinized him. Surely, the images trapped him in his room at night remained as transparent as the glass car he drove the night of the murder. His paranoia was growing. The conflict between the outward image and his evil undertakings coiled around him and squeezed.

Chapter Sixteen

They were partying atop the dead body

As spring unfolded in their sleepy little town, it got easier for Mike to focus on his life. He attended his senior prom and graduation parties—all the remarkable milestones in a teenager's life Trent would never experience. As the weather warmed, there was more partying to be done. Partying at the cabin on the farm held particular importance to Mike. Being the one with the prime spot for underage drinking gained popularity among his peers. The power burned a hole in their pockets. The power they longed for pushed the duo into telling.

If they did not articulate what they did, no one could hold them in awe of their prowess. They agreed not to involve any girls. Maybe they wanted to protect the girls in their peer group from the ugliness of what they did. Perhaps they assumed girls could not keep a secret. Or, maybe, they did not want to hurt their chances of dating a girl who possibly looked unfavorably at what they undertook.

The more Mike and Fred partied their way to the end of summer, the freer the secrets began to flow. Wouldn't more power, awe and admiration come their way if someone knew what they did?

Once Fred divulged their secret to his younger brother, it became easier to tell his brother's friends. Impressing the younger crowd, the partners fed off their awe of the crime. Mike and Fred basked in their new-found fame, and they created a rite of initiation into "The Boys." As part of the initiation into the crew, the cohorts disclosed the heinous events and swore the recruits to secrecy. The convincing was easy since Fred was known to always carry a handgun. He often boasted his gun was the murder weapon used against their victim, "The kid who went missing."

No problem securing secrecy. Fred used the weapon before. It could be used again.

Was it fear, loyalty, or disbelief keeping their secret quiet? Not one person who was in the know came forward to help solve the mysterious disappearance. No one considered allaying the agony of the missing boy's parents and family. According to court documents, at least ten young teens knew. The question of whether those boys ever mentioned the secret to their parents will never be answered. None of the ten came forward on Trent's behalf.

Summer marched toward its end, and all of the seniors partied away their last days of childhood on the farm, with Mike and Fred freely bragging about the killing. More than once, Mike or Fred stood outside the cabin under a big tree and declared to anyone in earshot that they were partying atop the missing Franklin High School senior.

Along the way, Mike occasionally wondered why Fred

deviated in the police station from the agreed-upon story they rehearsed together countless times. Every now and then, the inkling tugged at Mike's confidence.

Chapter Seventeen

He was torturing himself

The acceptance letter from the University of Georgia arrived, and Mike understood the importance of the moment. He chose the school because others he visited and applied to weren't enough of a distance from home. And it was far away from where Fred would attend the prestigious Virginia Military Institute in Lexington, Virginia. One would head south, the other north. Mike would run away to Athens and never look back. He fantasized it would be the easiest move of his life. He did not understand *The Plan* would follow him there. The distance would not be his miracle.

During the first year, Mike tried to live the typical freshman life—lots of social time, a little class time, and even less study time. Unfortunately, he could never strike a balance. It became not only easier but a requirement for him to stay in a particular altered state of mind through various ways of recreational self-medication. His new habits made getting up for classes laborious and eventually, unimportant. Quietly studying for a test was the equivalent of psychological warfare. He couldn't exist in silence. Loud music and drugs became the priorities of his daily life.

Mike left college due to bad grades after his first year. Those bad grades resulted from not going to class, stemming from the inability to live with himself. Plenty of times, he envisioned running away to a remote corner of the earth. He could never run far enough because the reality of what he did was a part of him.

He landed right back in Franklin, back in his mom's house. Defeated. He worked at a pizza delivery company and tried to distract himself from his disturbing thoughts. He befriended local kids either still in high school or who stayed in town after graduation. He balanced his self-medicating habits with intense video gaming and his job.

The irony of him driving the car with Trent's bloodstains still in the trunk weighed on him. Mike couldn't face cleaning it. He avoided opening the trunk at all costs. He refused to use it. No luggage, no athletic gear. Nothing. He was torturing himself.

Chapter Eighteen

Too much at risk for one of them to go off the deep end

After a year of being at home, Mike and his family agreed he was ready to return to college. Once the decision was made, he packed and headed back to Athens. The University of Georgia was willing to take him back. Besides, he still retained glowing references from prestigious names from his hometown, and for this reason they welcomed him with open arms.

Returning to his beloved college was a welcome change of scenery for Mike, but the same tortured state of being existed within him.

By now, his psyche was playing cruel tricks on him. He was convinced everyone in town, whether it was Franklin or Athens, suspected his dark deed. He waited for the sky to fall and expose him to his family and hometown. The unstable ground could open from beneath him at any time, sucking him into a bottomless free-fall forever. The signs constantly pointed to everyone knowing. The music on his radio told him. The movie choices others made exploited him. How people looked or did not look at him proved their shame towards him. The pair didn't keep their secret well after executing *The Plan*. How many told others? Why wasn't anyone telling those who needed to know? Two years passed since they committed the murder, and still, no one came to arrest them. Heading back to Athens to hide away seemed like his best option.

At UGa, Mike continued to placate his paranoia with recreational drugs to no avail. In social settings he presented the self everyone loved. And many peers embraced him at face value. Several nights, the self-medication loosened his tongue and lowered his self-esteem. If friends complemented him, he proclaimed to be an evil asshole. If no one took his statement seriously, he would divulge part of his secret by explaining he participated a in a foul thing in high school and was a very bad person. But the story contradicted his highly sociable, highly likable persona. No one agreed with him.

He suspected everyone saw right through him, and no one was bold enough to confront him. His paranoia taunted him from the shadows, slowly tearing him apart. He was off balance; his mind was sideways. Mike tired of holding in his secret and carrying the demon of truth on his back.

One night back in Franklin on a school break, Mike was having a bad recreationally medicated trip whilst hanging with friends. The group started watching Pink Floyd's movie "The Wall." The psychological drama involves drug-induced hallucinations and portrays a boy's lonely childhood after his father dies. The boy becomes a man, gradually losing touch with his sanity and the world as he builds a figurative and physical wall of protection.

Mike was sure every one of his peers was sending him a

message via the movie. They were onto his evil execution. Surely, they could see he was going insane. Mike could not make it through the entire film. He left the room at one point.

He called Fred often to let him know he was struggling with inner demons and paranoia. Finally, his most trusted friend told Mike to get off the drugs and persevere with his life. He urged him to smarten his act, adjust his life path, and forget what they achieved.

There was too much at risk for one of them to go off the deep end and talk. By now, Fred dedicated his focus on his ensuing military career. He excelled at VMI even in his first year as a "rat." The tough discipline at the school comforted him with the familiar feelings of how he was raised. Fred could not let Mike block his chances of achieving his dreams just because he was being weak and unsure.

To Mike, there was one way he could pull his life together. Confess. What would people imagine? How would they react? How would his mother take the news? Was suicide another option he could go through with?

As the shame, despair, and depression continued to grasp him, Mike again began to fail at college. He couldn't go back home to live. His mental stability was hanging by a thread. He needed a way out. Mike firmly convinced his mother the best course of action for him was to stay in

Athens for summer school. This would give him time to formulate his final plan. Once he finished summer school, he could go home and tell his family goodbye forever.

Mike was out of options.

If he turned himself in, he could not avoid implicating his oath brother. Their bonded relationship was failing him, and he no longer trusted it. His ever-growing anxiety was becoming a liability. He set his third option in motion.

It was August of 1992, and they still successfully hid their killing of their 17-year-old classmate, Trent Whitley.

By now, the partners lived separate lives. Mike, who was still struggling to hang in school, fighting enormous depression, fear, and paranoia, resided in Athens, GA. Fred was home for the summer after a successful year at VMI, where he received several accolades. With summer school completed, Mike returned to his Virginia home to set his plan in motion.

He announced to his mom and one of his brothers he was there to spend a few final days with them. He was leaving Franklin in his rear-view mirror, returning to Georgia to carry on with the rest of his life. He planned to drop out of college. Mike would no longer be in touch with them. They would need to carry on without him because he would never be back. He planned to close his loose ends, get as much of his stuff as he could fit in his car (the seats, not the trunk), and get his bank account together.

The reason suicide was not an option was because his dad was in heaven and if he killed himself, God would never let him see his dad again. He could not face the idea of this possibility.

Turning himself in and confessing to the evil deed accomplished two and a half years ago was a hard pill to swallow. He did not wish to disgrace his family. Besides, he did not like the idea of prison. Nope.

Permanently evading his old life and starting utterly fresh as a stranger remained his best option for all. Never setting foot on the farm where they buried Trent or the park where they abandoned his car sounded peaceful. Never again driving by the scene of the crime or socializing with Fred as they exchanged knowing glances pleased him. He would fade into the distant horizon and be done with the dark part of his life.

Of course, nothing he said to his family made any sense. What nonsense swirled in Mike's brain? How could he turn away from them and never come back home to see them? Not having any of it, harsh words volleyed back and forth between Mike and his family. The more Mike dug in his heels on the topic of leaving, the more obstacles his family threatened to put in his way to block him.

It seemed to be a passing conversation for Fred, but Mike noticed cracks in the cemented bond with his colleague. Was Fred's confidence in Mike shaking? He was battling the internal struggle of knowing what they did was wrong and the need to tell anyone who could remove the weight from his shoulders. Was it showing he was fortifying his coping with more alcohol and harsher recreational substances? Mike could feel himself spiraling downward but was certain no one could tell. His family suspected nothing sinister. His mood was as sullen as always. Surely there was no way their friends could tell. How would his best friend know he was in a constant internal battle not to tell anyone who could help him escape his complicated situation? How could anyone know he constantly flashed to the morbid cold night in his dreams?

By the summer of 1992 Fred could sense Mike losing control. He saw the spiraling and thought a night watching movies might help Mike regain his confidence. Being a student at VMI he loved military movies. He wanted to rent "Full Metal Jacket", but it wasn't available. He settled on "Apocalypse Now" starring Marlin Brando and Martin Sheen. The film opens in 1968 Vietnam, amid the Vietnam war. In short, the plot involves an evil genius, rogue Army Colonel Kurtz (Brando), who has gone off the rails. He and his recruits operate under full-tilt insanity, unchecked by the forces he rules. The assigned mission of special forces Captain Willard (Sheen) is to locate Kurtz and terminate him before the colonel can do more damage. An undercover soldier was sent earlier to assassinate the villain. Instead, the shell-shocked warrior joined Kurtz's maniacal village, falling under the spell of the cult-like leader. The movie is rife with drugs, guns, and countless killings. It is gruesome and violent. Fred picked the film for them to watch. Mike was quietly apprehensive, knowing its plot.

Talk about art imitating real life!

Mike knew Fred chose the movie to send a clear message. Mike was spiraling, and Fred needed to eradicate him because he morphed into a liability. Recreational treatments in hand, the duo watched the movie.

As the movie played, Mike hallucinated flashes of their horrendous deed, melding them with the actual scenes on the TV. The popping of gunfire triggered the intense blue flash and thunderous bang as Fred pulled back the hammer and ended Trent's life. The movie's portrayal of the treacherous Vietnam War brought the reality of dead bodies stacked in small villages to the screen.

For Mike, every dead body peered back at him with Trent's face frozen with the question of why. Because of his flashbacks, Mike struggled with the images in his mind. The paranoia set in, as Fred somehow transferred the homicidal pictures from Mike's mind onto the screen.

At the end of the night, as Fred was driving Mike back home, the two discussed the movie and the main characters. Fred unhesitatingly revealed he was, without question, Willard, the special ops assigned to exterminate the spiraling, mentally unhinged military liability.

Surprised at the revelation, Mike responded with the question of was he Kurtz. Again, without hesitation, Fred answered with a solid yes. No eye contact was made. No, "Ha Ha. just kidding." Only a hollow "yes," followed by an echoing silence.

Mike closed the car door in his dark driveway and Fred pulled away. Glancing in his rearview mirror Fred thought, *What? Are we in Literature class? I don't know what character I am.*

As Mike turned to walk inside Trent's voice echoed. "Maybe we can work something out," followed by Fred's hollow answer, "It's too late for that now."

Chapter Nineteen

He spewed his dark secrets

For weeks, Mike fixated on the movie and the conversation. He needed to find a way to mention to Fred again to determine his stance on who Willard and Kurtz represented. One day, Mike casually mentioned to his friend, "It looks like we committed the perfect crime since no one knows what we did except us."

Fred's rebuttal was, "No. The perfect crime would be to commit a murder and frame someone else for it."

What started as a pebble-size pock in a windshield now grew into a web of mistrust and doubt. The small chasm in Mike's confidence continued to spread the way Trent's blood spread in his trunk.

Knowing he was now in Fred's sights, he shifted into survival mode. Mike avoided being physically near his best friend. His choice was clear; he needed to disappear. Moving back to Georgia and starting a new life was the answer. Being away from Fred and away from the town where they murdered Trent would terminate the nightmare he created.

The turmoil with his family continued. Mike stuck to his plan of packing after the summer and moving to Georgia, never to return to his family or Franklin, VA. Mike told his family he would spend a few days at their beach house with a group of friends and he would leave permanently upon his return. His family agreed his going to the beach would give him a cooling off period, and held confidence Mike would come to his senses after spending time with his friends. Fred planned to be at the beach. While there, Mike intended to take time to let him know he was leaving forever and taking their secret with him. Maybe saying good-bye would convince his friend Mike was no longer a liability but was finally moving forward. In the back of Mike's mind, he built a fear of spending time with Fred. He couldn't help but reflect on the moments he and Fred differed in their intentions.

He started dragging his feet on the beach trip and focused on self-preservation. The more Mike avoided being wherever his friend was, the more Fred pressured him to go to the beach, offering to drive him.

One sunny afternoon, Fred arrived with his younger brother, unannounced, at Mike's house and told him to get packed because they were leaving in an hour to go to the beach. Fred's including another person in their plans was unusual.

The crosshairs pricked at Mike's back, knowing Fred plotted to kill him and dump his body on a deserted stretch of road along the way to their destination. This was a pivotal moment. Desperate to avoid Fred, Mike drove to a different friend's house, where Fred nor his brother would find him. Under the guise of being there to play video games and order pizza, Mike stayed late into the night until they left without him.

The following afternoon, he surprised himself by arriving at the family farm where one of his brothers, "Farmer", was working. It was a place where he felt unbearable fear and edginess, knowing Trent's body was still buried there. His mood was sour, which tried Farmer's patience. As brothers do, blunt words rushed between them. There was no sugarcoating Farmer's irritation towards his totally insane plan. How could he be so immature and uncaring? He caused their mom enough grief between how he treated her after their father died and his on-again-off-again relationship with college. Was Mike still not finished torturing their mom for the death of their dad?

Enough was enough! In Farmer's opinion, Mike was a spoiled brat and it was time for him to mature into a man. He wanted Mike to go to the beach for sun and fun with his friends and return ready to live life like a responsible adult. As Mike was ready to leave, Farmer mentioned he was planning to move his wife and daughters to the farm to temporarily live in the hunting cabin. The words stunned Mike.

In his mind his precious nieces accidentally stumbled across Trent's body as they played in the front yard. They would be terrified and scarred for life. How would it unfold? Would Farmer get blamed for Trent's death? Would they accuse him of Mike's doings? What would happen to those sweet girls if their dad went to prison? He could not let the scenario play out, so he spewed his dark secrets in one long breath. He dumped it all at Farmer's feet.

Mike demanded they could not move to the farm because Trent Whitley was buried in a shallow, unmarked grave by the hunting cabin. Because he was the one who put him there. Mike and Fred killed him in February 1990, buried him, and concealed the crime. He did not hold back. He unburdened himself but was met with stone-cold silence.

Confusion, fear, and disbelief riddled Farmer's face.

Mike experienced freedom in the intense moment. He was practically giddy with relief. Handing the blackness to Farmer induced euphoria. He decided to go to the beach first thing in the morning.

Mike would let his brother figure out how to deal with his secrets, finally untethering him from the heavy yoke he carried across his shoulders since his senior year in high school. He was ultimately hopeful for the future.

There was no way Farmer would stand in his way of leaving. Heck, he would probably help him pack. Mike was not living in reality. Farmer demanded there was no way he could go to the beach. He expected Mike to stay in Franklin and make things right. Mike was not in agreement with *The Plan* at all! Entirely disconnected, he swore his brother to not tell their other brother, the do-gooder, "Do Right", the one with the strict moral code. He was always making Mike do the right thing.

During Mike's senior year, he painted vulgar words and images on the barn silo across from the high school. Mrs. Jervey was appalled and embarrassed by her son's public artwork. Do Right drove two hours from his home to make Mike remove the vulgarities. The painting tradition was afforded to each senior class at the high school. Unfortunately, Mike took things too far by painting in bold letters an unsavory statement. Do Right came to do their mother's bidding as she no longer possessed the mental fortitude to deal with Mike's drama.

Farmer pressed Mike to tell Do Right with his own words. Either way, Farmer intended to have a conversation with Do Right. Deciding he would participate in none of it, Mike jumped in his car. He bid his farm brother farewell and tossed one last lob. Mike told Farmer to wait until he partied, packed, and departed before he told Do Right. He didn't want to be in the same room with him.

Mike left the farm to go prepare for the beach and get his party on one last time in Franklin. He would go see his friends in town and tell them he was headed to the beach for a few days of unwinding and partying.

Life was finally good again! He was finally free of *The Plan* and the darkness!

Mike spent the rest of his day and night in a lighter mood. He was so excited his master plan of escape and avoidance was working in his favor. He might make it.

Upon his 2am arrival home, after a night of partying and merriment, dread dropped on Mike like an anvil. Mike noticed two extra, yet familiar, cars parked in his mother's driveway. One belonged to Farmer and the other belonged to the dreaded Do Right. There was a wrinkle in Mike's plan, and with heavy trepidation, he entered the house. The brothers waited quietly at the kitchen table; their mother upstairs asleep. From the look in their eyes his grand master plan dissolved like seltzer tablets dropped into a glass of water. It was one thing to go at it with Farmer, but two against one was not going to be an easy conversation. Nevertheless, they talked throughout the night, and Mike accepted the New Plan as the sun rose.

Phone calls were made. Waiting occurred. There was a vast amount of silence - heavy, apprehensive silence.

They woke their mom and broke the news to her. They explained to her the New Plan. She needed to accept it. At one point in the day, Fred called from the beach, excited that Mike finally chose to join the beach group of party goers. He wanted to spend one-on-one time with him. Mike wavered. Fred was clearly upset at the news and seemed gloomy. Mike asked what was wrong; Fred expressed his sorrow over losing his best friend. Mike did his best to calm him and allay his fears. Mentally validating Fred's suspicions, he ended the call.

Mike exited the car in the parking lot of the police station. He turned and hugged his mom and his brothers, knowing their loving embrace may never surround him again. Every step forward brought dread and a longing to finally put an end to it all.

Chapter Twenty

Forever seventeen

Mike spent four hours unburdening himself of the sordid details of what happened to Trent. It was cathartic euphoria to finally purge the darkness from his soul. The words flowed like vomit from his lips as he spewed all the secrets, which haunted him for years, eating away at his sanity. The last part of his confession was taking them to find Trent's body buried on Mike's family's farm.

Handcuffed and sitting in the back of the police car, Mike flashed back to the cold night in February. He relived the ride he and Fred took with Trent's lifeless body in the trunk of his car. He remembered how the shock of the murder prevented him from maneuvering his shovel. The depth of what was happening pulsated through his body like hot lava filling him with terror.

He flashed forward to the sunny Sunday afternoon and could feel the sun's warmth in the crisp air. It was not lost on him how the comforting feeling diminished as he and Fred began the dreadful task of unburying Trent. He remembered touching the cold, sticky tarp encasing the body. His arms and back recalled the feel of them lugging the heavy corpse to its final home.

Thirty months passed since Fred and Mike left Trent's body in his shallow grave. Because so much time occurred, Mike's memory was not precisely on point. As he was let out of the police car, the scent of the damp earth hit him like a hammer sending dark memories through his mind.

The fragrance of wet dirt mixed with the metallic odor of Trent's blood in his memory. He led the police team to the general area on the farm, by the hunting cabin near the pond. It was easy to locate the first temporary burial site. However, trying to find the exact spot of Trent's final resting place was fuzzy. Mike did not pinpoint the precise location.

It didn't help that they were searching in the dark of night with flashlights dimly illuminating the wooded landscape.

For more than a week, a team of investigators and diggers worked at the site trying to locate Trent. The team was desperate to return him to his devastated parents. The lead detective in the case was dedicated and undistractedly focused on finding the boy.

Labor Day weekend came, and the heat and exhaustion overwhelmed the team assigned to finding Trent; the chief sent everyone home to recharge. The detective could not be swayed to stop looking. His frustration was mounting because of their lack of success locating the victim. He needed additional support.

He tapped into specialized experts and called upon Professor Bill Bass, a forensic anthropologist at the University of Tennessee – Knoxville. Mr. Bass founded the world's first Anthropological Research Facility, established in 1980, where the decomposition of human remains is still studied. The facility was later dubbed The Body Farm by Virginia crime author Patricia Cornwell in 1994. The detective contacted professor Bass and told him of their search for the body of a boy buried on a rural farm in Virginia two and a half years before.

Bass gave him the tips he needed to be successful, one of which was to partner with a local botanist who would understand the growth and change in local vegetation. The detective contacted a Botany professor at Paul D. Camp Community College in Franklin. The botanist agreed to meet the detective at the farm the next day. After informing the botanist what to look for, according to Bass, they got to work. Within two hours, they pinpointed a viable search site, and the detective went to work digging.

Bingo!

The body of Trent was finally found and carefully excavated from his cold, lonely grave. Of course, his body was not in good shape, making the removal tricky. Inside the makeshift grave, investigators also found Trent's empty wallet, driver's license, and the gold chain necklace he was rarely seen without.

Now, the detective faced the impossible task of letting Trent's family know they found their beloved missing boy. He formed a tight bond with the family throughout the investigation. Telling them would be a double-edged sword. While he finally relieved them of the agony of not knowing where Trent went, it was through devastating them with the finality of what happened.

At last, Trent was found.

The mystery of Trent's disappearance tortured his parents, family, and friends for thirty months. Finally, the adventure-loving boy who would be forever seventeen was going home.

Chapter Twenty-One

Unmoved by the apologies

"The past two and a half years have been the hardest years of my life… I wish there was something I could do to ease the pain."

Mike Jervey spoke these words to the court on the day of his trial as part of his apology to Trent's family and the community.

From the time Mike confessed until the day of his trial, Mike and his family received death threats. As a safeguard, authorities placed him in protective custody.

It was too risky for Mike and Fred to be in the same courtroom, so Fred's trial was held first. He received charges of capital murder, robbery, and the use of a firearm.

For the most part, the legal proceedings remained uneventful. He admitted to the execution of Trent, which took the death penalty off the table. He opted for a trial-by-judge, therefore there was no jury present. Trent's family and friends and a handful of reporters packed the courthouse.

The trial was a formality.

The district attorney went through the process of notifying the judge of the sorted details, which occurred in the weeks leading to and the night of Trent's murder. Within a few hours, the judge conveyed Fred's sentence, life in prison plus 62 years. He would be eligible to beg the parole board for mercy after 25 years of serving his sentence.

Mike's trial was next.

He was charged with first-degree murder and a firearms violation. Because Mike confessed to the crime and led police to the general area where Trent's body was buried, he was offered a plea deal to potentially shorten his prison time.

He was a bundle of nerves, knowing full well the judge could reject his plea deal and throw the book at him. Mike's attorney advised him the plea deal set his parole eligibility at 5 years and 2 months.

Mike was confident he could withstand such a short amount of time in prison. Surely the parole board would see Mike "handed" the police and Trent's family the answers on a silver platter. Thereby they would grant him parole upon his first attempt at freedom. Certainly, they would agree, until he voluntarily confessed no one ever knew about any crime related to Trent's disappearance. His family would still be searching for him if Mike didn't tell them where they buried him on the family farm.

Mike's trial was also presented to a judge. Again, there would be no jury to hear the details of his crimes. Similarly, the court proceedings seemed like a formality.

First, the judge listened to the district attorney as he described the events of Trent's horrendous assassination.

Within a few hours, the judge announced his sentence, 30 years in prison.

Given the opportunity, Fred and Mike apologized to the Whitley family. Fred apologized for the pain and anguish he caused and indicated he was genuinely sorry for his crimes. Mike went on further to say the dark secrets of his crimes overcame him and left him no choice but to confess. He ended with a Bible verse and the following statement, "God gave me the strength to come forward and confess my sins...by turning myself in, I know I've done what's right for everyone."

Trent's mother told reporters she was unmoved by the apologies and didn't trust their words.

The full transcript of the trial of Fred is available in the court files of the case. Suspiciously, there is no transcript of Mike's trial, confession, plea deal, or statement to the court.

During the legal proceedings for Fred, the district attorney chose not to submit Mike's police station confession to the court but instead summarized it as he described the evidence.

There is no transcript of Mike's taped confession or apology to the court.

The prosecutor did not charge the ten students who knew of the murder within months or years of the crime. They were 16-17 years old at the time of the trials. They all testified Fred told them at different times the story of Trent's homicide and Mike confirmed it at least once. Fred's younger brother showed some of the boys the gun. He let them know it was, in fact, the weapon used to kill Trent, according to the transcripts of the trial-by-judge.

We will never know precisely what was said in Mike's trial. No transcript from his murder trial exists with the Clerk of Court of Southampton County, VA. Mike's confession to the police was recorded. Still, it was never presented as evidence to the court, nor was a transcript found. The Franklin Police Department, the Southampton County Sheriffs, nor the Southampton County District Attorney's office maintain copy of Mike's recorded confession at the police station. Also, the official investigation file is no longer in the possession of those agencies.

The talk in the town after the trial was mostly about the preppy young tennis and basketball player from the local, prominent family. Most people assumed he became entangled in a wrong decision one night ending with prison time.

Trent's gracious, sweet mother stated in the press she empathized with the two other families over losing their sons. The press did not report public statements from the murderers' families. But where was Trent's moment? Still, today, the townspeople and classmates of the three boys talk in hushed tones to avoid any disparity towards the prominent family.

The high school yearbook usually has a dedication page devoted to a student or faculty member who was tragically lost too soon. Unfortunately, Trent never got a dedication page in his yearbook. He didn't get a dedication during the years he went missing, or once he was finally found in an unmarked grave on a family farm miles away from town.

Chapter Twenty-Two

Our inner voices were screaming

Our intentions of covering our hometown cases on our podcast has never been to disparage the town itself, but we are driven to tell the stories of lost lives. Regarding Trent's case, we tried to tread lightly because his is a story unaddressed in a public forum such as a podcast.

We dug deep because we are familiar with one of the families involved in the story. We knew the Whitley family, but we didn't know much information detailing Trent's life. Most of the folks we spoke to in the community, couldn't remember specific facts about Trent. They recalled the sensationalism of the confession and the trial. Either from fear, community loyalty, or allegiance to the families of the murderers, no one was willing to speak publicly.

The silence drove us harder to tell Trent's story. After all, our primary focus has always been on the victim.

We did our research as best we could and recorded the episode. As we told the story, we tried to stay neutral, aware Trent's family still lived in Franklin. We understood one of the murderers served his time and returned to live in the community. The pressure of our hometown reputations weighed on us.

We opted to make warm and gooey brownies for the episode. We made the brownies from scratch and narrated the case using court documents, newspaper articles, and stories passed along to us. We wanted to paint the picture of our hometown in the most pleasant way possible. The last thing we would want is for one homicidal act to define our community.

We labored to convey the images of our town—a great place to grow up or raise a family, where the community shares the importance of morals and values. Through our research of hundreds of cases, it has become evident murder has a ripple effect. Intentional homicide leaves a mark for generations on the perpetrators and victims as well as on their immediate and extended families, friends, and the community.

There seems to be an indelible scar imprinted from a murder, which never completely heals.

On August 21, 2021, we opened the following email:

"Hello. I hope all is well with you. I'm a producer working on a true crime series to air on the Discovery Plus network.

Our series focuses on...what happens when a terrible crime impacts a community —not only in the immediate aftermath of the tragedy but also for decades to come. As you mentioned in your podcast... the ripple effect of such crimes reverberates for generations.

I'm reaching out to you both because I listened to your podcast about that case with great interest. You are

both terrific storytellers, and the hometown/community
you brought to the story was compelling...."

_____

That is a lot to unpack.

First, did you read the part where a producer from Discovery Plus (an affiliate of the Discovery Channel) thinks we are terrific storytellers?

I mean, you had us at *Hello!*

Next, they are interested in a compelling story we reported.

The rest of the email continues with the pouring of more sweet sugar, and the producer ends with "Let's talk" and her cell phone number.

Who are we right now? We read it to each other and Googled the producer's name to see if she was real or imaginary. Sure enough, she was legitimate. From that point we did what any professional podcasters would do. We called everyone and told them a producer from Discovery emailed us expressing her admiration for our podcast.

Once we came off the sugar high, we replied to the producer and scheduled a time for a phone call.

The short and sweet of it is the network wanted us to narrate Trent's story as part of the series and use our ties to the community to get cooperation from the town.

We started making contacts and doing more research into Trent's case. We drove to Franklin and had conversations over lunch, dinner, and late-night drinks with people close to Trent's case. We were full throttle moving forward with the research. However, after a series of events, we mutually agreed to pull the project.

The case was not included in the series. We feel good with the outcome, although disappointed. We made appointments to get our hair and makeup done for TV and ordered slimming clothes to pop on camera.

The sugar high officially faded.

We learned a lot from the experience, and a slow-burning fire simmered within us. Our inner voices screamed at us to find a way to get Trent's story told. We pressed to recount his story in the best way to honor him.

We tucked away our notes and shifted our focus back onto the podcast, but those inner voices never wavered. Whenever we doubt ourselves, we go back and read the email from the producer. We remind ourselves how a producer from the Discovery network called us compelling storytellers at one point in time.

We returned the TV clothes but kept pictures in case more opportunities come our way.

Chapter Twenty-Three

Listening to the disembodied breath of God knows what

A little more than thirty days after the initial contact with the network producer, we received a shocking email.

The author shared how he appreciated the way we stuck to the facts and did not interject our personal judgment, especially regarding his family. Unbelievably, he agreed it is a tragedy his victim's memory has not been kept alive in the town.

Surprisingly, he offered to share a conversation with us regarding his case and how we portrayed it. Finding his correspondence unfathomable, of course we agreed to talk to him.

We did exactly what no one would expect us to do.

We bought a burner phone with cash from a local mom-and-pop store and booked a time to talk. On the day of the scheduled call, we drove to a random location and activated the phone for the call.

For weeks, we would repeat the procedure but at different locations. One time in a parking lot in the next town and other times in the parking lot of a bank or grocery store. We pulled into a graveyard once.

Our fear kept us moving and dodging.

Once the conversations ended, we would remove the battery from the phone and keep the battery in one car and the phone in another. We kept our calls completely secret from everyone. Picture two small-town, fifty-blank-year-old broads on a super-secret spy mission but totally afraid. Kind of like the Golden Girls on a James Bond 007 pursuit.

We took the opportunity to genuinely listen to what he said.

We needed to know where he was coming from in wanting to chat with us in our weekly confidential conversations. Was he plotting our demise? Was he interested in what we thought? What was his agenda?

In our discussions, we exchanged points of view on his case, honest in our opinions and respectful of his. Because he served his time and gave his due diligence according to the law by serving his sentence, we owed him no discrimination.

Needless to say, the small burning fire to tell Trent's story got stoked!

Our inner voices pitched a hissy fit. We're simple at heart. We don't see the need to complicate things. However, we set high aspirations which required a lot of research.

As part of our research, we went back to Franklin. The first stop on the way into town was at the county courthouse in the Clerk of Court office. We obtained the court files and engaged in a few interesting conversations with the employees who remembered the case. At first, they seemed tight-lipped speaking with the strangers from

SC. However, once we divulged our maiden names, the floodgates opened, and the information flowed.

Amazingly, one of our old childhood neighbors worked in the office and remembered us as little girls! Our next stop was at Franklin High School in search of yearbooks from Trent's Junior and Senior years. We wanted to see pictures of the friend groups of Mike, Fred and Trent's class and get a feel for what life at the high school was like back in their day. The librarian recognized us as hometown gals, and she allowed us to take the yearbooks we needed and return them later via mail.

We wrapped our first day with the most challenging meeting.

Late in the afternoon, we went to the park where Trent's car was found. We met with the lead investigator and one of Trent's brothers. The investigator answered our questions with reference to the case. He shared stories from his involvement with the investigation and interactions with the Whitleys. He added in a few details which we had not heard before. Trent's brother recounted the family's experiences in the days and months after he went missing and the final realization Trent was not coming back to them.

Although enlightening, the meeting was tough to get through without strong emotions—shock, horror, sadness, anger, and disbelief.

Discussing Trent's murder was no easier for them to get through than in 1990, the year he went missing, and on the day in 1992 the detective informed them of his death. By resurfacing these difficult times, the family and the community relived it again. But we left there knowing firmly Trent's story needed to be told in order for the rumors and speculations to be put to rest. He deserved to be more than a footnote. We were determined to find a way to memorialize young, innocent Trent.

On a future trip, the author of the email consented to meet with us face-to-face.

Before meeting with the author, we needed a concrete action plan—safety first. As true crime podcasters, we tend to overthink. Dark scenarios and suspicious characters are at the forefront of our imaginations. A conversation with our psychic medium friend yielded a list of five protection crystals we would need to carry in our purses and pockets. Next, we consulted with a police officer on how best to approach the scene. He adamantly told us not to go and meet with the mystery man. We went anyway. We didn't disclose our plans to our families because they would side with the police officer. Controlling the meeting and driving the conversation were our priorities. Setting the timing of breaks was key since we would need to stay hydrated and fresh.

As we parked in front of the secret meeting location, we

lit a twig of palo santo to clear our minds. We armed ourselves with plenty of cold water and cupcakes for comfort. As we exited the vehicle and spotted our interviewee our nerves kicked into overdrive. As a matter of fact, our nerves overcame us and we accidentally left our provisions in the car. Once inside the building, we walked into a small office. We took our seats and exchanged pleasantries and small talk. Did we hear him lock the door? We asked the first question—can you tell us about the night of Trent's murder?

Four and a half hours later, we exited the office into the daylight; we thanked our host and vowed to stay in touch. We never paused for hydration or freshening.

We listened like school children at story time, captivated and nowhere in control of the conversation. As our host turned to walk back inside, we exclaimed in union, "What did we do?"

Scared we might be seen or followed by an unknown predator lying in wait, we squealed tires. After driving for fifteen minutes in stunned silence, we stopped and simultaneously grabbed for the water and cupcakes. We frantically stuffed three cupcakes each into our mouths and gulped water. After the last swallow we spoke, noticing the crystals sitting in the cup holder.

As we drove to the AirBnB we rented in a different

state-again, safety first-we kept repeating to each other, "What have we done?"

Once at our accommodations, we had much to discuss. We unpacked and examined all the information we obtained on our trip and started taking notes. We talked into the wee hours of the morning, and as the sun broke the horizon, we surmised we possessed no ideas on how to write a book.

Being resourceful shoppers, we purchased several books on how to write a book. We read the books, highlighted sections, discussed the books in a mini book club atmosphere, and determined we still didn't know if we could write a book.

We're good at talking (gabbing, discussing, chatting). Instead of figuring how to write the book, we shared in depth conversations on what we wanted to say in the book. Once we settled on our content, we started looking for the perfect location for our writer's retreat. We picked an off-the-grid location in the mountains of North Carolina.

The hotel was described as an antique inn nestled against a granite gorge. Its claim to fame was many US Presidents frequently visited. Additionally, the lake across the street is where they filmed part of the movie, Dirty Dancing. The picture in our minds was the resort inn where a fictional Baby stayed with her family. Instead, we got a quaint little inn trapped in a time portal. While a tiny bit of memorabilia highlighted the famous stays, the main focus of the guests, unbeknownst to us, was the haunted rooms and areas of the hotel. We checked into the poltergeist inn; we traveled too far to turn back for home.

Tired from our trip, we wouldn't get much writing done the first night. The plan was to get to bed early and get plenty of shut-eye in an effort to be ready to tackle our endeavor first thing in the morning.

Needless to say, it didn't go well.

One of us was jolted from sleep by heavy breathing sounds in the vacant bathroom. As she lay there listening to the disembodied breath of God knows what, she needed to get her sister involved. It took several attempts to rouse her sister from her slumber.

It was 3 am, by the way.

Once the sleeping sister was awake, the scared sister explained the reason for waking her was a man was breathing in the bathroom.

The sleepy sister responded the best way she could. "Why are we having a full-sentence conversation at three o'clock in the morning? You need to go to sleep."

The haunting of our room was a hot topic between us the next day, but we managed to press ahead and get started. Our first order of business was breakfast. You need an excellent healthy, protein-rich breakfast to get those brain cells moving. After getting lost on many-a country road and having our life scared out of us by a passing bunny, we found the sweetest little roadside cafe and indulged in pancakes. We would try the protein thing for lunch.

Returning to the inn, we desperately needed naps as our sugar high from breakfast quickly dissipated. We awoke in time for lunch. You see where we are going here. After dinner, we got to writing! By Sunday evening, we wrote a mere 10,000 words between the two of us. The task was going to be more complex than expected.

We didn't leave the inn with an entire written novel, but we did meet many unique haunted inn characters. First, we convinced a couple to get into the crime scene clean-up business. *Who knew you needed a certification?* Another couple insisted on buying us multiple shots of liquor at the bar— we're not ones to turn away free booze.

It was a successful four days.

How naïve of us to undertake such a goal! Lots more work lay ahead of us.

After the initial 10,000 words, we began collaborating on a schedule, and the words flowed on their own accord. Many nights, Trent's presence guided and encouraged us to keep going and be confident in our mission.

Victims become mere footnotes in the stories of their untimely demise. We aren't featuring the stories covered on national television or recanted in the international media headlines. We are showcasing the victims quietly held in memoriam by family and a few friends but who are no longer discussed. We came to understand they need to be brought into the light and given permanence in their history.

This is our mission in starting the "Say My Name" series.

Chapter Twenty-Four

Say his name

W e never had the pleasure of meeting Trent in person.

We've done a great deal of research and participated in many conversations regarding Trent. Part of the conversations were for book research.

We still wonder how Trent seemingly got lost in the story of his own murder. There was so much focus on the assassins. Trent became part of the background and he deserved to be front and center.

Truthfully, the more we told the story and researched the details of Trent's case, the more the small-town boy, forever in high school, became part of our family. He's our little brother now.

Trent deserved to be laid to rest appropriately instead of being left on a random family farm to rot in an unmarked grave with students partying on top of him.

We wrote Trent's story because we wanted to give Trent his moment. He deserved the happy graduation from high school with the pomp and circumstance he earned as a popular, grade-A student. He was due to date girls and maybe get married and enjoy the experience of babies. He merited happy birthday celebrations, Christmases, Easters, hunting, fishing, and all the joys life has to offer.

We are the sisters who want to shower him with the recognition and remembrance he never received. Mr. and

Mrs. Whitley's son waited in the lonely, cold grave through springs and winters, summers, and falls, to be found and laid to rest by his adoring parents and brothers. He now rests next to his mom, who passed away years after these events. He is also joined in heaven by one of his older brothers. We are sure they are together as they should be. We know one of his brothers goes and visits Trent and Mrs. Whitley every day. He misses them both and often ponders why no one speaks of Trent anymore. How could such a sweet, deserving boy get forgotten in his own murder?

WE WANT TO CHANGE THE OUTCOME. PLEASE, AS YOU FINISH HIS book, take a moment and say his name:

Raymond Trent Whitley

Raymond Trent Whitley, Franklin High School Yearbook

First article about Trent missing – Tidewater News, Franklin, VA

What happened to Trent Whitley?

Family still hopes for his return after vanishing nearly a year ago

Trent Whitley

Article on 1-year anniversary of Trent disappearance – Tidewater News, Franklin, VA

News of murder of Trent Whitley, naming arrests; picture inset is Fred Greene leaving his arraignment – Tidewater News, Franklin, VA

Mike Jervey leaving arraignment – Tidewater News, Franklin, VA

Family desires to bury son

☐ Continued From Page 1A

"We almost didn't expect to ever hear anything. We figured this might always be a mystery to us. Then out of the blue, it was so unexpected."

Sitting in the family's comfortable living room in their home on Clay Street, Delores said, "If Mike Jervey hadn't come forward, we still wouldn't know."

Now the Whitley family is wrestling with the biggest question — why did this happen?

"I would like to know the motive," she said. "We still have questions, but we are trying to understand why the police are keeping the information quiet. I think that's good in a case like this.

"They have kept things under wraps and I understand and agree."

She said the barrage of questions and requests from the media has not been too bad.

"The first couple of days, the television people were here or calling all the time. But they were real nice about it. They weren't pushy."

She added that all the media have been good about honoring the family's request and channeling questions through family friend and local attorney James E. Rainey.

Delores recalled that Trent was not close friends with Jervey or co-defendant Frederick West Greene, but said they knew each other, they were acquaintances.

It was a friend who informed the Whitleys the names of the pair arrested for their son's murder.

"It was a total shock," she said.

One aspect of the case has been particularly difficult for the Whitley family to handle — the incessant rumors which have circulated since the first posters about Trent's disappearance began appearing in store windows back in February 1990.

Delores said, "I've heard all the rumors, especially ... tried to down play that.

"I never saw Trent on any drugs and if he was, he was a good actor. I never saw anything.

"I hope I'm smart enough to recognize the signs. The worst part of that is his name has been dragged through the mud over this.

"We even heard he was the biggest drug dealer on the East Coast."

The Whitleys also didn't believe the persistent rumor early on that Trent simply ran away, even though they filed missing person and runaway reports with police so the information could go across national police wires.

"He knew he could have come to us if he was in any trouble. He knew he might get 'blessed out' by us, he knew he could still come to us.

"We never knew he was in any trouble."

Even though it has now been two weeks since the arrests, Delores is not sure if the full impact has hit the family yet.

"There are a lot of different emotions going through all of us right now. We try not to dwell all the time on what happened.

"We still go to work or do household chores, the boys go to work and I think it has been good for us to do that," she said.

James "Bunk" Whitley is vice president and co-owner of R.L. Tillett Inc. in Franklin, Doug is a dealer in rare comic books in Tampa, Fla., Scott is an exterminator in Burlington, N.C. and Kirk works part-time at a Franklin McDonald's.

Delores said, "I still go to the grocery store, we still have to have clean clothes. It's a matter of trying to maintain as normal a routine as possible.

"I sometimes feel that if I really start crying, I may never stop. So a regular routine helps. We cry, don't get me wrong, we do cry. But, we are trying to be strong."

Even with the pain and sorrow her family is feeling, Delores still has compassion for the families of the two accused ...

Family addresses murder and rumors – Tidewater News, Franklin, VA

Officials silent on search

Dog teams come, go — no results

Officials search for Trent's body – Tidewater News, Franklin, VA

Police find murder weapon in Fred's home – Tidewater News,
Franklin, VA

*Whitley portrait (Mrs. Delores Whitley and her sons) – Tidewater
News, Franklin, VA*

Union Camp car wash – no photo credit

Franklin High School Barn and Silo painted – no photo credit

Trent at a formal dance – Franklin High School Yearbook

What's done in the dark always comes to the light.

Jesmyn Ward

Acknowledgments

First and foremost, we would like to thank our family, Darren, Sarah, Noah, and Cameron. Thank you for your unconditional love and your in-your-face critiques, good and bad. We appreciate your forgiving us for all the shenanigans, most of which were incurred while writing the book.

We love you all to the moon and back times infinity!

Thank you to Andrea, one of our biggest cheerleaders, our spiritual fairy godmother, and the only person to ever attempt to get into our heads to wrangle and organize our thoughts.

Thank you to our countless friends who believed us when we said we were going to write a book and waited patiently for it to finally materialize.

Thank you to the Sugar Coated Murder podcast community for continuing to listen and encourage us.

The Authors

Karen and Anne are sisters who grew up in a traditional family home in the 70s and 80s in Franklin, VA. They both attended colleges in Raleigh, NC—Anne at Peace College, and Karen at Meredith College —where their sisterly bond began to flourish.

They enjoy reminiscing the quirky events of their childhood, especially their antics as teenagers in a small town. Their love of baking was born in their Momma's kitchen and their humorous style of storytelling was honed with the humor of their father.

Now, they are both professionals by day and podcasters by night. Their podcast, Sugar Coated Murder, is a combination of baking, true crime, and of course dark, inappropriate humor.

Made in United States
Orlando, FL
16 March 2024

44848143R00100